5 POWERS THAT LEAD TO FULFILLMENT

Richard Tiller

5 POWERS THAT LEAD TO FULFILLMENT

Richard Tiller

Pentland Press, Inc.
England • USA • Scotland

PUBLISHED BY PENTLAND PRESS, INC.
5122 Bur Oak Circle, Raleigh, North Carolina 27612
United States of America
919-782-0281

ISBN 1-57197-154-8
Library of Congress Catalog Card Number 99-068272

Printed in the United States of America

This book is lovingly and gratefully dedicated to my wife, Chris. I am thankful that we had the opportunity to pursue our individual paths to fulfillment together.

Contents

Introduction

Before jumping into *Five Powers that Lead to Fulfillment,* let me address two questions:

1. What is fulfillment?

2. Why am I writing a book about it?

We experience fulfillment when we believe in ourselves and in our purpose—when we believe our life has value. The belief that our life has value provides us with a feeling of contentment, a satisfaction with ourselves, an inner peace that is the essence of fulfillment. Just as the verb "to fulfill" means "to satisfy," it also means "to complete." Fulfillment comes partly from the sense that our life has been made complete, that we have not squandered it meaninglessly. We feel fulfilled when we believe we have made the best use of the opportunities life has offered us.

At the opposite extreme from fulfillment is emptiness—a void within our soul that comes from feeling our life has no value, purpose, direction, or focus. It is a sense that life is pointless and futile. We see this emptiness expressed in the despair of the writer of Ecclesiastes when he declared, "All is vanity."

From where does fulfillment come? Why do some people find it so easily while others struggle with its elusiveness? Why do some people feel enriched by their lives while, as Thoreau said, "The mass of men lead lives of quiet desperation?" Was fulfillment intended merely as a gift for a select few?

We have all been sent an invitation to a life of fulfillment. Yet we often struggle with the decision of whether or not to accept the invitation. The decision should be easy, so what makes it difficult?

When I say we have been sent an invitation to a life of fulfillment, I mean we have all been given five powers we can use to achieve fulfillment. The struggle comes in deciding *whether* to use these powers, and then *how* to use them. Like any other power, the five powers that lead to fulfillment can be used, neglected, or misused. Abusing these powers is like abusing any other power, leading us not to fulfillment, but only to disappointment and despair.

Understanding these powers is the road map to fulfillment. Using them is the road itself. This book is about choices—about how to make positive use of the five powers in order to make the most of life's opportunities. The fact that our choices can determine our fulfillment is one of life's most exciting challenges.

The five powers we will explore throughout this book are:

1. THE POWER TO CHOOSE YOUR REACTION

2. THE POWER TO CREATE

3. THE POWER TO RECREATE YOURSELF

4. THE POWER TO GIVE

5. THE POWER TO INFLUENCE

Each of these powers leads to its own kind of fulfillment. More important, however, is the way the powers work together. They are an example of the whole being greater than the sum of its parts. They are arranged in the above order to show how each one leads to the next, and to enable us to study the relationship between them as we go. "The Power to Choose Your Reaction" lays the foundation for the rest of the powers, while "The Power to Influence" ties them all together.

Developing these five powers takes patience, perseverance, courage, and honesty, but the reward is tremendous. It means that our fulfillment does not depend on luck or circumstances, but on our use of these powers. We know this from seeing some people who are at peace in adversity while others are miserable in prosperity.

These five powers are not gimmicks or secrets for success. In fact, fulfillment and success can be quite different. Success can lead us to fulfillment or away from it, as we will see. I am not claiming these are the only powers that lead to fulfillment. They are based on observations from the work I do, which leads me to the second question raised in the beginning: Why am I writing a book about fulfillment?

I work as a consultant to salespeople who sell new homes for builders, and also as a consultant to their managers. New home sales is a profession that offers a lot of fulfillment or a lot of frustration, depending upon the salesperson's attitude and approach. My job is to help them maximize their successes, and their career fulfillment. I am hired to train and counsel people in a stressful occupation filled with unexpected challenges. All my work with salespeople and managers is one-on-one in the field. This allows me to see up close how a variety of people achieve their own fulfillment in a demanding profession.

Success for new home salespeople comes from a combination of skills and attitudes. The fulfillment they receive from their profession is an entirely different matter. Naturally, if the skills are never developed and success is never achieved, it is unlikely that salespeople will ever find fulfillment in their careers. However, for those who do develop the skills, what is the real source of their fulfillment?

The five powers play a vital role in the personal fulfillment of the people I coach, and I see these same powers leading to fulfillment elsewhere. My goal is to observe and learn ways that the most fulfilled salespeople and managers use their five powers, and then use this knowledge to help other people develop their own powers. Here is a general overview of how I see salespeople make use of each of their five powers to achieve fulfillment.

The Power to Choose Your Reaction

Salespeople who achieve the greatest fulfillment make their own choices about how they will respond to various successes, failures, and challenges they face. Knowing they cannot choose the events they will confront on a day-to-day basis, they do the next best thing. They choose their reaction to those events in a way that sets the stage for the best long-term results from those events. In the face of adversity, they adopt the role of problem-solver rather than victim.

The Power To Create

They see themselves as a creative resource. They create their own strategies and techniques to pursue their objectives and address challenges.

4

THE POWER TO RECREATE YOURSELF

They recreate themselves to adapt to new companies, markets, communities, product lines and clienteles. The environment and challenges of a new home salesperson can change quickly, dramatically, and frequently. Many salespeople have recreated themselves in order to enter the profession in the first place.

THE POWER TO GIVE

Salespeople who achieve the greatest fulfillment over the long haul are more often givers than takers. Being a successful and fulfilled salesperson does not have to mean being a taker, nor does a giving spirit produce a weak salesperson.

THE POWER TO INFLUENCE

Naturally, the power to influence is important in selling. But on a higher level, the kind of influence that brings salespeople true fulfillment is the kind that elevates the environment around them, enriching the lives of their co-workers and customers.

Many salespeople and managers with whom I have worked, along with other wise people I have known or studied, have provided the inspiration for this book. As I discuss the five powers in greater detail, I will be using illustrations (real and fictional) that extend beyond my profession. I hope this book can convey what I have been able to learn from others and apply in my own life concerning the *Five Powers that Lead to Fulfillment.*

1
Power To Choose Your Reaction

Earl dreamed of owning a trucking company from the time he was a child. Many little boys are fascinated with trucks, but Earl's excitement continued to grow. By the time he was a teenager, he had already begun to envision a trucking empire. His trucks would haul freight throughout every state in the country. He would not give his trucking line a fancy name. He would just call it Earl's. Earl's trucks would carry anything everywhere. If you needed something shipped, you would know to call Earl.

Earl did not have money. Yet he knew if he could save enough to buy his first truck without a loan, he'd be rolling. He could borrow money later in order to grow, but he wanted to get established with cash. He didn't want to start off in debt.

Saving for that first truck took longer than Earl expected. The savings grew slowly while truck prices kept soaring. After working as a courier, a cab driver, and at a few construction jobs along the way, Earl finally landed a job driving for a trucking company. He drove for years, living frugally in order to save his money. Hundreds of dollars grew into thousands.

He was thirty-two when he got his chance to take the next step. His employer agreed to sell him one of their older trucks.

It took time to find his first client. He did not want to go after his employer's customers. At last he found a business willing to hire him for a delivery, so he left his job to incorporate Earl's Trucking.

The shipment looked like a great opportunity—a big load to carry over two thousand miles. The first day of travel went smoothly. Earl's Trucking was a real company headed for big success.

On the second day, snow began to fall. Earl hoped he would get past it, but the snowfall kept getting heavier. Visibility grew worse and the road became icy, but Earl kept going. As the danger increased, so did Earl's determination.

Darkness fell, and the wind blew harder. It was nearly a blizzard now, yet still Earl refused to stop. That night his truck skidded on the ice, crashing sideways into an overpass support column. Earl's injuries were minor, but his truck and the freight were destroyed.

Earl was covered only by liability insurance. He had taken the risk of running his first delivery with no other insurance. After years of driving without any kind of misfortune, he felt his decision was well calculated. He had planned to buy insurance with the profit from that first shipment. He could have waited a little longer in order to save up for more insurance, but the lure of a live customer with a big order was too tempting. After waiting so many years, one shipment without an accident did not seem so much to wish for. Worst of all, he had lied to his client, telling them their freight was insured.

In just two days Earl was ruined. His old company was sympathetic and hired him back, but his lifelong dream had ended on a patch of ice under a bridge.

The other truckers didn't say much to Earl for a couple of weeks. They mostly left him to himself, because they knew how much he had sacrificed to buy that truck. They realized that after years of dreaming and skimping, his tragedy was greater than any of them could imagine.

Earl was glad to be left alone, and he seemed to be doing all right. Eventually, a close friend decided it was time to talk.

"How are you holding up?" the friend asked.

"I'm okay," Earl answered.

"That's good," the friend replied, feeling frustrated. He didn't know what else to say. Finally he spoke up again. "I know that truck was your dream. If you need anything, I'm here."

Earl looked down for a moment. Then he looked back up and just said, "Thanks."

As the friend got up to leave, Earl stopped him.

"I put everything into that business. My whole life has been about Earl's Trucking. It's all I lived for, all I thought about. But it's strange. For the first time in my life, I'm really free. I can be whoever I want to be. Nothing can hold me back any more."

One of life's greatest frustrations is not being able to choose what happens to us. Yet one of life's greatest blessings is the fact that we are all given the power to choose our responses.

We cannot always choose the events that invade our lives, but we can always choose our reaction to those events. The power to choose our reaction to events means we can control the ultimate effect these events have on our lives. This ability to control how events affect us is an extraordinary power, unique to humans among all creatures. The more we think about this power, the more exciting it becomes.

It is a gift to us all. It has nothing to do with our circumstances, and nothing to do with our intelligence. It has to do with our internal choices.

Internal choices are different than external choices. External choices are those that are limited by external forces, such as circumstances or other people. Choosing between three job offers would be an example of an external choice, because someone else is telling you what choices you have. Internal choices are the ones in which you choose how your circumstances will affect you on an internal level. Once you make your external choice from among the three job offers, your internal choices determine how you adapt to the new job and how you maximize whatever opportunities you are given. While external choices are limited by forces beyond your control, internal choices are entirely within your control, because internal choices involve the way you think.

After the accident, Earl's circumstances limited his external choices. He could not go out and pay cash for another truck. He did not have the ability to borrow money to restart his business. Even if he could get funding, he might never be able to win customers again. Customers will always have plenty of other shippers from which to choose—companies that haven't destroyed a client's freight their second day in business.

While Earl's external choices seemed discouraging, his internal choices gave him hope. He could not choose what had happened to him, but he could still choose its ultimate effect. He realized that while his previous direction had been destroyed, his ability to choose his future direction had not been. His destiny still lay in his internal choices. His future still belonged to him. He had lost his trucking business, but he had not lost the power to choose the ultimate effect of his failure. He could still use the power to choose his reaction to create a new future as rich and exciting as his last one. No one could take that from him except himself.

The power to choose your reaction is a wonderful gift not because it can improve your circumstances, but because it can improve the ultimate effect of your circumstances.

Bad events offer as much positive potential as good events. Both can be used to shape a positive future direction. Events are often viewed as bad when they are unpleasant, undesirable, or inconvenient. They are seen as good when they are pleasant, desirable, or convenient. But the power to choose your reaction is what often determines whether the ultimate effect of an event will be good or bad.

Neil was a professional golfer who had focused his entire career on winning the U. S. Open. He committed years of practice and sacrifice to become a champion. Finally, at the age of twenty-eight, he achieved his goal and won the U. S. Open. Like Earl, Neil fulfilled his greatest dream. He became the champion he always believed he could be.

The next year, another young pro named Alex won the Open. He had followed the same path to success as Neil, practicing and sacrificing and dreaming for years. It all paid off for Alex, just as it did for Neil.

Five years later, Neil was still winning major golf tournaments. He was one of the greatest golfers in the world, respected wherever he went, and happy with his life.

Alex, on the other hand, dropped off the professional golf tour altogether. He developed a drug problem; his wife left him; he could not find work anywhere because of his reputation for being difficult and irresponsible.

Neil was asked, "What was the beginning of all your success?"

He answered, "Winning the U. S. Open."

Alex was asked, "What was the beginning of all your troubles?"

Alex answered, "Winning the U. S. Open."

Was winning the U. S. Open a good thing or a bad thing? The ultimate effect of winning the U. S. Open was determined by how Neil and Alex each reacted to his victory, and what direction each took as a result. History is full of champions in every field who use their victories either as springboards or anchors to their futures. Why do some successes lead to greatness, while others lead to self-destruction? Clearly it was not the circumstance of the victory. The victory was the constant. The variable was the reaction to the victory, and the choices following the victory that shaped the future direction.

What about tragedy? The principle is the same. Divorce, loss of employment, death of a loved one, a debilitating disease or crippling accident are all devastating tragedies. These kinds of traumas have destroyed many lives, yet propelled others to greatness.

A doctor loses a spouse to disease, and this tragedy inspires a commitment of years of work toward discovering a cure for the disease. Was the death of the spouse a bad thing or a good thing? Obviously, we would consider the death a bad thing. The better question to ask would be whether the ultimate effect was good or bad. The doctor chose a reaction which produced a wonderful ultimate effect.

Suppose the doctor had not found a cure. That is not really the issue. The issue is that we have the power to choose our outcome—to choose how things will affect us. The doctor made a conscious choice to use adversity—a devastating personal tragedy—to set the most fulfilling direction for the future.

It is not your successes or failures that set your course in life, nor is it the good things or bad things that happen to you. <u>It is your reaction to these events that will guide your future</u>. This is a fascinating dimension of the human experience.

It is important to understand how great and vital your power to choose your reaction can be for achieving long-term success in life as well as personal fulfillment. In fact, the power to choose the ultimate effect of the events in your life can also enhance each of the other four powers you have for achieving personal fulfillment.

◆ ◆ ◆

Life does not always follow our original plan. It often turns out better.

When life detours from your plan, your reaction determines the ultimate effect of those detours. It sets the stage for the new direction your life will take. Often this new direction offers surprises more wonderful than anything your original plan could envision.

Having a plan sets a starting point for your direction, even though you won't have the power to control the course of events as you pursue that plan. This is a frustrating limitation, but one for which to be grateful.

When we first conceive of a plan, we are missing many important pieces in the puzzle of our future. We cannot know all the possibilities the future holds. So a plan can only be a starting point.

Sticking with a plan requires commitment, fortitude, patience, and self-discipline. Many people abandon their plan because they cannot tolerate the setbacks or hardships. Often, their plan just doesn't work out as they expected. Health, finances, or conflicting responsibilities can interfere. Maybe the plan was ill-conceived in the beginning. Sometimes a better opportunity comes along.

The failure of a plan is not ultimate failure. In fact, the opposite is often true. The ultimate effect of a failed plan may produce greater success and fulfillment than the original plan could ever have delivered. This has been the case for me.

With a bachelor's degree in cultural anthropology and a strong background in literature, my goals were to pursue both of these directions until one panned out. I felt that by pursuing Plan A (anthropology), Plan B (teaching English), and Plan C (a career in publishing), I couldn't miss. One hundred thirty-five job applications in all three areas led to as many rejections.

I had never imagined a career in sales, but I decided to try new home sales in an effort to make a living until I could find a "real job." To my astonishment, I enjoyed home sales, and then marketing and management, and now training. A quarter of a century later, my career has provided me with far more fulfillment than I had ever dreamed possible for any of my original plans.

I eventually learned that in order to gain real fulfillment from my work, I would have to invent a career for myself. I believed that new home salespeople and managers needed one-on-one training as well as group training, so I became the first person in my field ever to train full-time and nationwide on a solely one-on-one basis. It was a difficult profession to start, since the concept had no track record and, therefore, no credibility. After eight years, it has become the most fulfilling career I can imagine.

My career was not something I could ever have planned. I would not have known enough to imagine it. It simply evolved.

My family situation is the same. After my first marriage failed, my second one has been a wonderful blessing. I had planned to have natural children, which time proved impossible. Instead, I have two stepchildren, now grown, who have been as great a joy to me as I had ever imagined natural children could be.

When a plan is not working out, the decision of whether to stick with it is a case-by-case judgment call. There is no universal formula. We can only weigh the risk, the effort, the potential, and the options.

We always have options. Sometimes the options do not seem as appealing as our original plan. Yet these modest fallback plans can often lead to new directions with greater potential than our grand original plan.

How can we keep ourselves moving in a positive direction when failure seems to push us backward? Begin with the idea that failures occur in order to lead us to greater successes. *Loss can be the beginning of opportunity. Failure is not bad, and it is not permanent. It is only inconvenient. Good results take time. Long-term, big-picture thinking is critical to achieving fulfillment.*

We have all heard the expression of a glass half full referring to one aspect of positive thinking, just as we have heard of a glass half empty relative to negative thinking. It is one of those little clichés that embodies an enormous principle.

Perceiving the glass as half full, not half empty, is one of the most important attitudes for achieving fulfillment. I see this principle in action every day in my work with salespeople and managers. The glass-half-full people with whom I work gain more satisfaction, happiness, sense of purpose, and usually more success than glass-half-empty thinkers. They also suffer less frustration and anxiety, and handle adversity much more effectively. The distinction is worth a closer look.

Earl the trucker saw his glass half full after his business failed.

Glass-half-full people are excited about what will come next, while glass-half-empty people expect the other shoe to drop. Glass-half-empty people get stuck in neutral worrying about what could go wrong. Glass-half-full people keep moving forward, assuming that if something goes wrong it can be fixed. They are not reckless or impulsive; they simply believe in themselves and in the wealth of opportunities life has to offer. They establish their own momentum and then keep it going. Glass-half-empty people often stall, then look to their surroundings instead of themselves for a jump start.

I mentioned the fact that glass-half-full people handle adversity more effectively. This is because they view it from a different perspective. Glass-half-full people view adversity as a springboard, while glass-half-empty people view it as an anchor. To glass-half-full people, bad things lead to good things. Adversity leads to opportunity and is a source of many triumphs. Crisis is an opportunity for greatness. Life is a series of adventures, experiences, and wonders. The end of each experience is the beginning of a new one.

Everyone has the choice of being a glass-half-full person or a glass-half-empty one. In fact, it is one of the most important choices we will ever make. But it is not an easy one. Choosing a glass-half-full mentality may take a lot of thought, will, discipline, and time. But as this mentality develops, we see the difference in our overall feeling of fulfillment.

Developing a glass-half-full mentality requires us to step outside ourselves in order to objectively observe our own reactions. We can check ourselves from time to time by asking, "Am I thinking glass half empty or glass half full?" Then we can ask, "In what direction will my current thought process take me? Am I establishing momentum that will move me forward, or am I losing momentum that will leave me stuck?"

Let's look at a few more examples of differences between glass-half-full (GHF) thinkers and glass-half-empty (GHE) ones.

GHF: They look for the good in other people.

GHE: They look for the bad in others, being constantly critical.

GHF: New situations are opportunities for success.

GHE: New situations are opportunities for failure.

GHF: Competition is an opportunity for victory. They think about winning. They believe they will succeed.

GHE: Competition produces the risk of defeat. They think   about failure and are frightened by it.

GHF: They focus on their past successes as a source of confidence for future successes. Some even keep a running record of their successes for occasional reflection to boost their confidence and energy level.

GHE: They focus on past failures and, therefore, have less confidence in the likelihood of future successes.

GHF: A closed door means go on to the next door.

GHE: Closed doors are dead ends.

GHF: Life will continue to get better. Tomorrow will be better than today. They are eager for what lies ahead.

GHE: Life will continue to get worse. Today was hard, and tomorrow will be even harder. They are fearful of what lies ahead.

GHF: Aging is an enriching experience.

GHE: Aging means deterioration.

GHF: Every person is innately powerful.

GHE: Every person is innately weak, except for the few lucky ones who are powerful. Circumstances and luck are the most powerful forces of all.

GHF: They find security in themselves.

GHE: They find security in others (or in favorable circumstances).

GHF: Criticism is an opportunity to improve. It is not threatening, because critics are not perfect either.

GHE: Criticism is a put-down.

GHF: Rejection is a signal that something (or someone) better lies ahead.

GHE: Rejection is defeat. It is a step backward. It is humiliating and produces self-pity.

GHF: When they want something they realize they cannot have, they find contentment with what they do have or pursue something else.

GHE: When they want something they cannot have, they feel deprived and angry, and are jealous of those who have it.

GHF: They view their problems within a larger context. (How much of my life does this problem really need to take up? After all, there is much more to my life than this problem.)

GHE: Problems dominate their lives.

GHF: On the seventh day of a ten-day vacation, they say, "I have another four-day vacation, and it begins today."

GHE: They say, "This vacation is almost over. Time to get ready to go home and back to work. What a disappointment!"

GHF: If an unexpected delay or conflict causes them to miss an opportunity, they assume they are being saved for a future opportunity that is better.

GHE: If they miss the same opportunity for the same reason, they are angry because they lost out due to bad luck.

Glass-half-full people tend to be more energetic. Optimism is energizing. If we believe it will be a good day when we first wake up in the morning, we hop out of bed ready to go. If we convince ourselves it will be a bad day, we are likely to lie there staring at the ceiling as the minutes tick away. We will struggle to gather the energy to pull ourselves out of bed.

Thinking about the future can exhaust us or energize us, depending on how we anticipate it. The future can be our friend or our enemy. It can be a source of hope or fear. We get to choose.

Each morning as we awaken, our first thought might be, "I can choose for today to be a good day or a bad day. Which do I choose? What will I do to make my choice a reality?"

We may know from what is already on the agenda that it will be a difficult day. But that is not the same as a bad day. The most difficult days can produce the greatest triumphs and often the greatest fulfillment. Anybody can coast through an easy day. Heroes and champions triumph on the difficult days. You can choose how you will approach the difficult days. Your choice will have an enormous impact on your energy level. When the glass is half full, energy is higher.

An example of a choice we all have to make is our attitude about the weather. Dreary, rainy days can be discouraging, even depressing. Just looking out the window on a rainy day can be enough to sap our energy. We cannot choose whether or not it will rain, but we can choose how we will respond to the rain. This choice can have a lot to do with determining what kind of a day it will be for us. First, we must decide whether rainy days depress us or energize us.

During the time I was working on this chapter, I drove from my home to a client's location about four hundred miles away. It was the Sunday after Thanksgiving, so traffic on the interstate highways was very heavy. Road construction closed roads down to one lane for long stretches at a time. It rained the entire distance—often hard and accompanied by high winds. It was a very long drive, the kind of experience that can become oppressive and discouraging.

A difficult drive is not a life-shattering tragedy. Compared with real tragedy, it is quite trivial. But it is a commonplace experience. True catastrophes are rare for most of us. Over time it is our reactions to the day-to-day inconveniences that subtly shape the larger direction of our lives. It is probably more important for us to learn the glass-half-full approach to the everyday obstacles. If we can maximize the potential in life's minor opportunities and challenges one day at a time, we will be better equipped to handle the major ones.

After about an hour of driving in these conditions, I began to feel demoralized. I had left at two o'clock in the afternoon expecting to reach my destination by nine. At the rate of the first hour, it would be midnight before I arrived. What a miserable way to spend ten hours! The normal drive of seven hours on a beautiful day was bad enough.

Soon I found myself getting discouraged about more than just the drive. I began to feel lonely, wanting to turn around and go home. I no longer looked forward to working, which was dramatic, because I love my work, and I especially like the client I was on my way to meet. Before long, my whole life began to feel futile and pointless. All this just because of a little rain. And my spirits at the start of the day had been great.

As I sank deeper into this funk, I caught myself by saying, "Wait a minute. This is exactly what you're talking about in the chapter you're writing now. Okay, so this is a difficult drive. It is inconvenient. That doesn't make it a bad thing. Whether this drive is bad or good is my choice. Do I want it to be an enjoyable experience or a miserable one?"

Once I remembered it was within my power to make it an enjoyable experience, I had to ask myself how I would do that. First, I had to remind myself that in the big scheme of things, a drive that would take three hours longer than usual was not a crisis. A lot of events get delayed by three hours, including some of my own plane flights.

Next, I had to think of some potentially positive benefits of my situation. For one thing, I could enjoy the rain. After all, rain is a beautiful, fascinating phenomenon. Then there were the clouds, with their intriguing shapes changing by the moment as the wind pushed them across the sky with surprising speed.

I had more time to think and pour some of my thoughts into a tape recorder. What should I think about? Past successes. The vision of future successes. All the good things that have happened to me in the past year. Pleasant thoughts about my family. Since it was the end of the Thanksgiving holiday, I could reflect once more on all the things for which I could be thankful.

In terms of external conditions, the drive did not get any better. It took the full ten hours. Yet the drive became delightful, relaxing, and productive. And I had the additional satisfaction of knowing that my potentially bad experience became good because I had decided it would be good.

This is a simple example of choosing between a glass-half-full and glass-half-empty mentality. Yet many of life's experiences are like that—ordinary events that we choose to make either good or bad. We make our choices as these events unfold. Our choices determine the ultimate effect of the event.

Severe tragedies—divorce, death of a loved one, loss of a job, a crippling disease or accident, or other major setbacks—are naturally much more traumatic. While I do not mean to equate a drive in the rain with life's greatest tragedies, I believe the principles for dealing with them are essentially the same. Once we accept the setback of the tragedy and go through the necessary grieving process, the next step is to seek out the positive potential within the adversity, then make a positive decision as to how we will move on. A setback is an opportunity to pursue a new direction or to make improvements in our current one. After the initial traumatic grieving is done, the grief evolves into a new direction that fills the void produced by the tragedy.

Comebacks are one of the great triumphs of the human spirit. When a person achieves success, then sinks to rock bottom and returns again to success, we see something magnificent. We see one of the finest examples of the power to choose our reaction—to choose how events affect us, to determine the ultimate effect of a traumatic adversity.

Jean had established herself as one of the outstanding novelists of her generation. During a time when action thrillers and stories about doctors, lawyers, politics, and crime dominated the world of high-profile fiction, Jean's stories were exceptional because of their depth and sensitivity. The development of her characters throughout her stories provided profound insights that her growing audience hungered for and found refreshing. Her books radiated warmth and hope. They were stirring. When her readers finished them, they felt uplifted and satisfied. She drew richness from her own struggles growing up on a farm in Oklahoma with her widowed father. She and her father adored each other. Together they shared the adversity of financial setbacks and the experience of surviving them simply.

After her third successful novel in five years, Jean's recognition and wealth led her into a faster-paced world than she had known in her first thirty years. It was a world filled with different people and experiences than those that had shaped her earlier world. By her mid-thirties, she had developed a hard-edged cynicism that eroded the quality which had made her writing exceptional. Her stories lost their warm, uplifting sensitivity—the notion that every person had a unique and special value.

With two mediocre novels over the next three years, she began to lose her audience. There was a growing feeling within her as well as her readers that her flame had burned out. More importantly, her work no longer brought her satisfaction or fulfillment.

Jean realized what had happened, and she chose to fix it rather than mourn it. She set about turning back her clock. She thought about what had made her a successful and fulfilled writer in the first place. Realizing that the uplifting warmth and hope had disappeared from her stories, she turned her imagination to the circumstances and values that had brought her the greatest satisfaction in earlier years. In her mind's eye, she relived the life that had been the source of her greatest work. She created characters that embodied those attitudes. She then created a story around those characters that rekindled her spiritual vitality. This book was her most successful ever. Many of her former readers returned, bringing new ones who were fascinated with the idea of an artist recapturing her former inspiration. Jean's sense of fulfillment was not only renewed, it reached a new height because she realized what she had accomplished by reviving a gift she feared she had lost forever.

Recapturing a former excellence and then surpassing it is an exhilarating achievement. Comebacks are an exciting example of choosing a glass-half-full mentality over a glass-half-empty one. They require a special kind of energy that a glass-half-full mentality produces, just as moving on to achieve greatness in a new direction does.

Salespeople face the challenge of comebacks frequently. New home salespeople are often responsible for one community at a time. They sell that community for awhile, then move on to a new one. Switching to a different community often requires significant changes in style and strategy. They may be forced to change major elements of their sales approach, and this can take time. During the period of these new changes, their success (and therefore their income) may temporarily decline. Fighting the frustration and discouragement of these situations requires the kind of big-picture, long-term, glass-half-full thinking we have been discussing.

In addition to changes in their environment, salespeople must contend with seasonal slow-downs and personal slumps. They must make their comebacks again and again. They succeed by first assuming they will succeed. They view setbacks as opportunities to build upon their foundation of previous successes and to grow to an even higher level of excellence in the future.

Another difficult choice we sometimes face concerns the challenging issue of forgiveness. When someone hurts us in either our personal or professional lives, we often want to hold onto it. If we forgive the offender, we absolve their guilt. This does not seem fair, because we think they deserve to suffer for what they have done. If we suffer and they don't, an injustice has been done. We have a need for justice. They should suffer at least as long as we do. Forgiving them just seems wrong.

Yet if we do not forgive, it will likely do more harm to us than it will to them. It will probably prolong our own suffering more than it will theirs. So the injustice will be increased, not resolved, by our unwillingness (or inability) to forgive.

When we are hurt, forgiving is our greatest victory, because there is power in forgiveness. Forgiving the enemy raises us to a higher level in the relationship. When we forgive enemies, we free ourselves from their power. We make the choice of not giving them any true power over us—that is to say, no power over our minds or our spirits. They may still have political or authoritative power over us, but they have no power at the more significant spiritual level. This is important, because it is at the spiritual level that true fulfillment lies.

On the other hand, when we choose not to forgive, we increase the offender's power over us. We allow the offense to eat away at us, making the ultimate effect of the offense even worse. We deprive ourselves of the freedom and peace that forgiveness provides. We allow the enemy to sleep better at night than we do.

Forgiveness produces greater spiritual power than revenge. The need to avenge keeps us embroiled in our adversity. The power to forgive releases us from it. By releasing ourselves from adversity through forgiveness, we free ourselves to move on. The adversity is no longer an anchor.

What about the offenders? We cannot control their reactions or feelings. We can only control our own. We can focus on the principle that forgiveness releases us, raising us above the situation and our enemies.

Anger and jealousy work the same way as vengefulness. All three of these emotions are powerfully destructive forces. The choice to cling to anger, jealousy, or vengefulness can be devastating to our personal fulfillment.

The end of an intimate relationship can sometimes provoke all three of these emotions—anger, jealousy, and vengefulness. It takes courage and fortitude to set these emotions aside in this type of traumatic situation. But releasing ourselves from these emotions is what allows us to continue on the path to our own fulfillment. Moving on is what keeps our momentum alive.

In cases of severe betrayal—in our personal lives or in the workplace—we are bound to hold onto our anger for awhile. There is nothing weak or unhealthy about that. But even in these cases, we cannot effectively pursue our own well-being and fulfillment until we eventually release ourselves from the anger.

When I talk about forgiveness, I do not mean allowing ourselves to be trampled. We can still be aggressive in defending ourselves or achieving victory over an enemy. When we have the opportunity to stop an offender, then, of course, we should. But once the offense has occurred and is over, then the decision to forgive becomes the important issue determining ultimate effect and personal fulfillment. Will we be more fulfilled by clinging to the anger, hurt, or jealousy, or by letting it go?

Injustice is one of the most difficult kinds of adversity. We are forced to handle being a victim of something that was unfair—something we believe should never have happened to us. The principles for handling injustice are the same as we have been discussing throughout this chapter.

Injustice can be devastating. Anger and grief are natural reactions. Both of these emotions can accompany the unexpected death of a loved one. But where do we go from there? Eventually, we must make the decision whether to feel joy for the blessings the loved one provided or regret for what was left incomplete. If we choose joy for what was as opposed to remorse for what was not, we wind up more fulfilled by the relationship, and the legacy of the loved one has greater value.

A very frustrating injustice might come in the form of an unfair boss at work. Many people struggle with abusive supervisors who torment them and ridicule their work while taking credit for their accomplishments. If the boss feels threatened by the employee, he or she may eventually drive the employee out of the company altogether. Again, anger is appropriate for a while. Then comes the time to decide that working for that boss, or for a company which would tolerate that kind of boss, was not the best path to personal fulfillment anyway. The better path still lies ahead. Now the employee is finally free to find it.

An injury forces the end of one career and the pursuit of a new one. The second career taps into a new gift that had never previously been used or perhaps even discovered. Fulfillment is now gained from two successful careers instead of one—an even more satisfying accomplishment.

A demotion leads an employee to a position at which he truly excels. Although he may earn less money and have a less prestigious title, he finds greater fulfillment through his success and enjoyment at the lower position than at the higher one. For the first time in his career, he has found a source of gratification greater than money or titles.

A person handles a slanderous accusation with dignity. It takes some time for the accusation to be disproved. But once it is, the victim has a better reputation than ever because of the opportunity to show grace and courage in a situation of excruciating anxiety.

All these are examples of ways fulfillment can be achieved through injustice by the person with a glass-half-full mentality. A glass-half-empty person in the same circumstances runs the risk of sinking deeper and deeper into self-destructive despair by resigning himself to the role of victim.

Unfortunately, many people enjoy the role of victim. It attracts attention and sympathy, which can feel good. Sometimes it can even be profitable, if exploited effectively through the media or the court system. These avenues are not necessarily wrong. They may enable the victim to correct (or at least be compensated for) the injustice that has occurred. But the role of victim can never lead to fulfillment.

You might use adverse experiences to help others through similar experiences. Other times, it is better to put adversity behind you and move on. Just remember that it is a choice; you have the power to control the ultimate effect of your adversities.

Equally important are the choices that control the ultimate effect of your successes. Many people are subconsciously more frightened by the prospect of success than the prospect of failure. That is one of the reasons people sometimes self-destruct in the face of success. With success comes the responsibility of managing that success and maintaining its level. For some, the responsibility and the spotlight are too heavy a burden. There is nothing wrong with this, but it needs to be thought through in advance. At what level of success does my true comfort level lie? How much success do I want the responsibility for managing? The unbridled pursuit of success can lead people away from fulfillment instead of toward it if the success is not managed effectively.

In pursuing success, the first thing to do is define what you believe success really is in each area of your life, and how important achieving it is in those areas. People who plan their success one step at a time are often the ones who gain the greatest fulfillment from success in the long run. They use time as their friend instead of their enemy by taking as much of it as they need to grow into their success.

They master each stage of their personal success before moving onto the next. They envision their limits in advance, and they don't compromise their values in order to exceed those limits.

Summary

The journey toward fulfillment begins with choices. Sometimes these choices are difficult. Choosing one alternative often means sacrificing other opportunities that you are not ready to relinquish. Yet the courage to make these choices and the wisdom to make them correctly are what keep life moving forward on the path to fulfillment. This book is about how to make the right choices in using your *Five Powers that Lead to Fulfillment.*

You cannot choose all of the events that will occur in your life, but you can choose how these events will affect you. While you cannot always control what happens to you, you can control the ultimate effect of what happens to you. The choices you make in how you react to the events in your life are just as important during the good times as they are in the bad times. You need to control the ultimate effect of your triumphs as well as your adversities. Adversity often offers as much potential for fulfillment as success, and success can lead you away from fulfillment just as much as adversity can. It all depends on the choices you make about your reactions.

Loss can lead to the beginning of a new opportunity—a new road to fulfillment—if we are open to it. We need plans to keep our lives moving, yet life often detours from our plans. We can view these detours as new opportunities that perhaps offer more potential for fulfillment than our original plan.

In this chapter, we explored differences between glass-half-full and glass-half-empty thinking in choosing our reactions to the events and circumstances of our lives. We saw how long-term, big-picture thinking causes us to choose reactions that produce better ultimate effects for both triumphs and adversities.

The power to choose your reaction is just as important in the small day-to-day ups and downs as it is in the dramatic, life-changing ones. Choosing your reaction to mundane events (such as inconvenient weather) helps shape your life in subtle ways, a little bit at a time. Over time, these small choices also train you to discipline your thoughts and channel your feelings when tougher choices and challenges confront you. Even in those emotionally charged times when it is impossible to control your feelings, you can still choose how to respond to those feelings and handle them.

We saw examples of choosing reactions in the cases of Earl the trucker, Neil and Alex the golfers, and Jean the novelist. I also discussed my own choices for a new direction after failing to find success or fulfillment in my original one. In each case, the ultimate effect of a success or failure came from the power to choose your reaction.

This chapter examined how glass-half-full thinking can change the course of misfortune. It then expanded the idea of such thinking to choices involving forgiveness and injustice.

There are many events in our lives that we don't fully understand, but that's okay. We don't need to control or make sense out of everything today. Often, the events in our lives make more sense after time passes and we have a chance to see these events as small pieces in the larger puzzle of our lives.

Life is a series of adventures, experiences, and wonders, each one leading to the next. When you exercise the power to choose your reaction, you choose the ultimate effect of each event in your life. Will it be a springboard that propels you to new opportunities and fulfillment, or an anchor that drags you down so you lose the hope and energy to reach for the opportunities and fulfillment that are waiting for you?

Fulfillment is an infinite commodity, and it is there for the taking. The only limits are imposed by you and your own decisions regarding how the events in your life will affect you. Glass-half-full, long-term, big-picture thinking increases your possibilities and with them, your potential for fulfillment.

2

POWER

TO

CREATE

Dee Dee's Restaurant was casual, but the food was great. It made a nice gathering place for a small town, and business was decent. Still, after six years, it seemed to have leveled off. Another newer restaurant had siphoned off some of the business, and the local economy wasn't growing. Dee Dee was holding her own, but she hoped that somehow better times would come.

Anne waited tables at Dee Dee's, and worked three nights a week at the bar. She was a good listener. People felt good about themselves while they were talking to Anne. On slower nights, she would listen to her customers' problems, ideas, and dreams. Anne did not have a terrific imagination, and she was not brilliant. But she was interested in the people who talked to her, and she gave them encouragement. This meant a lot to her customers. They wanted to know what she thought. With Anne, people could just talk things through. She became a trusted friend to many of the townspeople who came to Dee Dee's.

Word got around about Anne. Though she had been in town only a few years, she made friends easily. People enjoyed being around her. Her interest and encouragement energized them.

The nights when she worked, the bar always drew a bigger crowd. On the nights she handled tables, customers would ask to sit in her section. Soon, people began calling and meeting her outside of work just to talk. She was married, but her children were teenagers and her husband didn't mind. He appreciated her ability to help people, and he was happy to share her.

People thought of her not as a busybody, but as a caring person. She became a networking resource for all kinds of needs, personal and professional. People would ask if she knew anyone they could call, and she knew which folks in town were willing to lend a hand.

Dee Dee realized Anne's value to the business as well to her customers. Anne and Dee Dee went to the same church, where Dee Dee was involved in the church's needs ministry. Over time Dee Dee realized ways her restaurant and her church could work together as a resource for helping people. Dee Dee's Restaurant got the boost in business she had hoped for.

She offered Anne the opportunity to buy in as a partner if she could raise the money. One of the wealthier customers Anne had encouraged during a tough time agreed to loan her the money. She became a partner and Dee Dee's Restaurant continued to prosper.

Anne was not an artist or a genius. She never thought of herself as a creative person. But she discovered a way to create and to make it count for herself and the world around her.

Creativity is the ability to add something to the world. When something exists because of you that would not have existed without you, that is your creation.

When we think of creativity, we often think of artists (painters, sculptors, architects, writers or musicians). We naturally think of their creations as the works of art they produce. Art is certainly one example of creativity. But creativity does not just mean being artistic. The concept of creativity stretches much farther.

Anne's creation was perhaps less tangible than a painting, but no less important and no less creative. She created a way to help people and to help a business at the same time.

We are all creative. When a person says, "I'm just not creative," he is not just selling himself short, he is depriving himself of one of life's most enriching sources of fulfillment. It is an example of glass-half-empty thinking.

Each day we exercise our power to create. Our thoughts, actions, accomplishments, and contributions are creations that enrich our lives and the lives of others. We create our own fulfillment. The more we can exercise our unique creativity, the more fulfilled our lives will be. When we discover our own unique creativity, we unlock one of the doors to our own special place in the world—our identity and our potential greatness. If your creativity is not yet apparent to you, it is well worth seeking.

Certain types of creativity (especially in the arts) may win greater public recognition than others, but that does not mean they are greater gifts. Just because a certain type of creativity may temporarily be in higher commercial demand does not necessarily mean it is more fulfilling. In fact, fame and fortune can sometimes work against fulfillment because of the pressures and distractions that accompany commercial success.

There are many ways to be creative on a daily basis. Writing letters, decorating a home or office, planting a garden, preparing a meal, training a pet, resolving a conflict, suggesting an idea to help your office run more smoothly, helping a friend solve a problem, helping a child with homework are accomplishments requiring creativity and resulting in feelings of fulfillment.

We think of creativity in terms of Beethoven's music, da Vinci's art and ideas, or Edison's inventions. These are fulfilling creations, but so are carefully constructed business plans or well-planned social gatherings. Salespeople experience the satisfaction of creativity when they develop a new way of demonstrating a product's benefit or solving a customer's problem. Exercise and fitness create a better body and often a more enriched spirit. Many opportunities for creativity fall within our reach.

We can seek out small opportunities for creativity as well as large ones, and treasure each opportunity when we find it. Exercising our individual creativity is vital to achieving fulfillment in our lives.

When we get trapped in a reactive, crisis-management kind of existence where we don't have the time or energy for creativity, we surrender one of our greatest gifts. Enjoying and nourishing our individual creativity helps give our lives the value and fulfillment for which they were designed. Every person on earth was designed to enjoy creativity.

If you feel you are not creative or are unsure where your creativity lies, here are several questions to consider.

♦ What are some of the things you have done in the past that you felt were original or different? How were they different? Did the fact that they were different give you satisfaction? Could you call these activities creative?

♦ Of what accomplishments in your life are you most proud? How did creativity play a part in these accomplishments?

♦ What kinds of activities have brought you fulfillment in the past? Could you call any of these activities creative? Could you spend more time pursuing these activities? Could you pursue any of these activities as an occupation?

♦ When you allow your mind to wander, what do you most enjoy thinking about? In what ways are these thoughts creative?

♦ Ask other people who are close to you if they feel you are creative and in what ways. Ask them what they think makes you different or special.

The first three groups of questions deal with the past, while the last two focus on the present. Allow me to give an example of how reflecting from my own past on the first three helped shape my later direction.

At the boarding school I attended from eighth grade through my senior year of high school, some of the seniors were elected by the students to be prefects, a position of authority over younger students on the corridors where the students' rooms were located. Each corridor had one prefect. The corridor assigned to me was mostly students with poor academic records, poor disciplinary records, or both. It was considered the most challenging corridor in the school, housing the most rebellious group of students.

The primary way to administer discipline was through demerits. The first day of school I called a meeting with everyone on the corridor to announce that I would not give any demerits that year to anyone on the corridor, no matter what he did. I would simply trust them, and I asked them to trust me in return. Next, I explained the rules for the corridor, along with a list of special privileges that would be awarded to the group as a whole if everyone abided by the standards. If any individual ignored the standards, the group would be denied a privilege.

We were a team—all for one and one for all. I treated everyone on the corridor with respect, regardless of their past reputation. This respect was reciprocated.

Whatever challenges the students faced, I tried to help them on a one-on-one basis. I would also ask for their help with my own challenges.

Respect, dignity, and support became themes for the life of the corridor. At some level, most people, regardless of their past, appreciate respect, dignity, and support. This turned out to be just as true for the loners as for the friendlier ones. Morale and goodwill continued to improve as the months went by. By the middle of the year, we had all become good friends.

Our school was set up on a three-semester system. For the final semester, our corridor had the highest grade point average and the best disciplinary record of any corridor in the school. Again and again, students told me it was the happiest year of their lives up to that point.

Like Anne the waitress, I am average when it comes to creativity. Yet I had created an environment where the boys in my care could grow both in their accomplishments and their self-esteem. I now see the connection between the fulfillment I received that year and the fulfillment I receive today working one-on-one with salespeople and managers. I was seventeen then. The mistake I made was in waiting twenty-three more years to go through the exercise of asking myself the questions I listed above.

You may find opportunities for creativity in your career. However, if your work does not provide you such opportunities, there are many other avenues. Some people exercise their greatest creativity, make their most important contributions, and achieve their highest fulfillment outside of their careers.

In what ways can you be more creative in your family life? When a parent makes up a bedtime story for a child that entertains but also teaches lessons, it is a valuable form of creativity.

What about creativity in your other relationships? What talents extend beyond your work? What can you contribute that is uniquely you? These are your creations.

Let us first consider creativity in our thought processes. After all, our thoughts are our most frequent creation. Some people use a tape recorder or journal to help them direct their thought processes along a productive path, as well as to keep a consistent record of their creative thoughts.

It does not take a genius or an artist to enjoy and be enriched by the gift of creativity. I gain a lot of joy from the times I set aside just for thinking. Creating the time to think can be a challenge in itself. Create your thinking time proactively. Don't get caught up in a stimulus-response existence that deprives you of these enriching moments. Setting aside time to think on a frequent basis will enrich your life.

Getting the most out of your gift of creative thinking means taking charge of your thought process, instead of letting it take charge of you. So often our own thoughts trample us, beating us down as we give in to the darker side of our thought process—pessimism, hopelessness, depression, and despair. We all experience negative thoughts, but we do not have to indulge these thoughts or surrender to them. We can see them for what they are— enemies—and treat them as we would any other enemy. Too often we befriend our negative thoughts.

I find myself most vulnerable to negativity when I am lying down, especially at night or in the morning. When that happens, I find that the longer I lie there, the more powerful my negative thoughts become. Yet when I get up and begin an activity, my energy is restored and my negative thoughts dissolve. I then have no trouble going back to sleep or going on about my day.

Conquering negativity may require some experimentation. For me, lying in bed trying to willfully think positive thoughts does not work. Activity is what works. It took me a long time to figure that out. But now my negative thoughts are much less powerful, because I know I have a way to overcome them.

You can train yourself to get the most out of your creative thought process. You can choose whether your thoughts will be a springboard or an anchor. The difficulty so many people have is that they do not believe this is true. It is a self-fulfilling prophecy. If you believe you can harness your thought process and direct it toward fulfillment, then you can. If you don't believe it is possible, then you can't. This is where will and discipline come into play.

Why am I spending so much time discussing mental discipline in a chapter on creativity? Your ability to manage and direct your thought process helps you to make the most productive use of your power to create and get the most fulfillment from it.

Training your mind to get the most out of your creative thought process can begin by answering these questions:

♦ What do you want to think about? (You have the power to choose what you think about.)

♦ What do you want your thinking to accomplish? How can you use your thinking to improve your quality of life and lead you to a higher level of fulfillment?

♦ What do you *not* want your thinking to do to you? For example, you do not want it to lead you down a path of negativity that leads to hopelessness and despair.

Managing your thought process combines the power to create with the power to choose your reaction. One of the greatest challenges in thought management is maintaining order in our minds and lives amidst the variety of hurdles we confront and objectives we pursue each day. We want to keep the pressures and frustrations of one situation from affecting everything else.

Remember that you already have control over your mind. You do not need to search for that control. You need only to exercise it. Here is one way to do that. Imagine that your mind is made up of cylinders, all of which are separate and sealed shut. Each situation in your life has its own cylinder in your mind. It stays in that closed cylinder until you decide to open it in order to deal with that issue. You open only that one cylinder. The others stay sealed. You deal with that issue the best way you can in the time available. Then you put that situation back into its cylinder and open another. You never open more than one cylinder at a time, so no situation can ever spill over into the other cylinders. The key to this process is realizing that you control the cylinders.

When a challenge strikes unexpectedly, you may need to deal with it at once. Keeping all the other cylinders in your mind sealed, you go about the business of dealing with the new challenge to the best of your ability. When you have done all you can with that challenge, even though it is still not resolved, it goes into its own cylinder where it is sealed and stored until the time comes to reopen it. You then open a new cylinder to address a different challenge or objective, or you choose to keep all the cylinders shut for awhile and just relax.

This may sound like a terribly oversimplified approach to mental discipline, but the fact is that many people have mastered this type of approach to problem management in one form or another. The cylinder approach happens to be my own.

One of your most important creations can be a vision for your life. What do you want your life to be about? Why do you believe you were created? What do you have to offer? How do you imagine yourself?

Creating a vision for your life takes courage. Some people do not create a vision for fear of the responsibility of fulfilling it. After all, what if fulfilling the vision is simply not possible?

Creating and fulfilling a vision requires the same kind of discipline as any other creativity. This discipline includes the kind of thought management we have been discussing. Set aside time to create your vision. Think it all the way through. This kind of creativity is not freewheeling and reckless. It includes organization as well as hard work. Discipline and perseverance are important to long-term success in any endeavor. Creativity is no different. It requires commitment and perseverance to provide long-term fulfillment. I have certainly found this to be the case in creating and fulfilling my own vision, as I will describe in a few moments.

Creating a vision often requires faith. There are many obstacles that threaten any significant vision. In addition to courage, discipline, and perseverance, you need to believe in the vision and your ability to accomplish the vision.

Creating a vision for our lives takes the kind of long-term, big-picture thinking we discussed earlier. There are times when adversity makes the vision grow dim, and we struggle to keep it alive. This does not mean we have to cling to the original vision at all costs. It is okay to revise a vision when circumstances or new desires change your direction. The new vision will probably be better. After all, change is part of the creative process.

Creating your life vision takes a correct balance of patience and impatience. Patience to endure adversity must be combined with the impatience required to take initiative.

Just as creating a life vision requires all of the characteristics described above, fulfilling it requires the same ones. Fulfilling our vision often takes longer than we want it to, and the path to it is often tougher. But it is worth the journey if we can develop and maintain the attributes of courage, discipline, faith, big-picture thinking, and the correct balance of patience and impatience.

Creating and then fulfilling a vision begins with three steps. The first step is simply to dream. What would you do with your life if you had no restrictions and knew you could not fail? Imagine a life that you believe would bring you satisfaction, contentment, and fulfillment.

The next step is to envision your dream—to begin to give it form. Here is where you start filling in the details. At this point you are considering not only the possibilities, but also the restrictions. What are the factors that could keep your dream from becoming real? Are those factors insurmountable, or are they merely inconvenient? If they are truly insurmountable, then go back to step one and allow your mind to follow a different route to a new dream, one you believe you can realistically achieve. Evaluating all the obstacles takes honesty and courage. Is the journey through those obstacles worth it?

Envisioning is one of the highest forms of creativity. It does not require the mind of an artist or a musician. Athletes from baseball players to pole vaulters often create a vision of their endeavor before they execute. Many salespeople envision a sale before they make a

43

presentation. The principle of envisioning increases success in any pursuit.

The third step is to create a plan for bringing the vision to life. Create your long-range plan first. This plan must be general enough and simple enough that you can follow it all the way through in your mind (or on paper). Now you can set about filling in the details of the plan as completely as possible with the knowledge you have. If you need more knowledge to fill in these details, then the next stage in creating your plan would be to acquire this knowledge.

I talked earlier about my one-on-one consulting business with new home salespeople and managers. Let me describe how my vision for that business evolved.

I never really developed a true life vision until I was forty years old. I had goals, but no vision. Without a vision, goals can remain vague and distant. However, when I turned forty, I began to think about which parts of my career had been most fulfilling and which had not. As a sales and marketing manager for a home building company, my greatest joy and fulfillment came from mentoring people individually. I wanted more time to help them meet their challenges, grow their careers, and find their own fulfillment through their work. I felt tremendous satisfaction when people who worked with me achieved success.

What I enjoyed most was working one-on-one with salespeople in the communities where they sold the homes our company built. However, the higher I moved up the management ladder, the less time I was able to spend on individual mentoring. I realized I wanted to go no higher than the vice president position I held. This was when I first began to create a vision of the kind of career that would be ideal for me. Only at this point did I finally make the connection between my joy of one-on-one mentoring and the boarding school experience I described earlier. Suddenly, all the pieces began fitting together for what my future direction should be.

I began with the dream stage. What I really wanted was a career where I could devote myself entirely to mentoring salespeople and managers on a one-on-one basis. Next, I began to envision myself performing this function. I literally envisioned myself doing the kind of coaching I had done as a manager, but doing it on my own with salespeople and managers as clients instead of employees.

The problem with my idea was that it had never been pursued as a full-time career. All of the full-time sales trainers in the home building business taught in a seminar format. There was no such thing as a full-time one-on-one sales coach, as there is in athletic professions such as tennis, golf, ice skating, or track. The occupation, therefore, had no credibility in my industry. This was the greatest challenge threatening my vision.

I began to develop a specific plan for creating a career where I could exercise my own unique gifts and skills. First, I would need a vehicle to give me credibility. I decided the best way to accomplish this would be writing a book that would allow me to share my thoughts on selling. My first book was called *Success in New Home Sales*. It served as a learning tool for salespeople and also to let prospective clients know where I stood. My books and newsletters on training and management came out later.

Next, I knew that in order to build a career that could eventually become full-time, one-on-one field work, I would have to start by offering a combination of seminars and one-on-one training. The reason for this was that there was already a high demand for the seminar style of training. It was a known commodity and was considered cost-effective. I started out offering a package which combined group seminars with one-on-one training. In the beginning, the cost of the one-on-one portion was minimal. My plan was that once I was able to establish credibility for the one-on-one field training on a trial basis, I would eventually be able to focus on it exclusively. Fortunately, no one else in the industry was interested in performing the one-on-one training, because it is considered riskier and less lucrative than seminar training. Plus, with a seminar format, the trainer has more control and can repeat the same program again and again. Field training that is tailored to the needs of individual salespeople requires versatility and spontaneity.

I started out with seminars in order to fulfill the expectations of the market. At the same time, I increased my skill and experience on the one-on-one level. The one-on-one concept began to catch on because salespeople enjoyed it more than group training. They told their managers they benefited more because we were able to devote our time to their specific needs that would help them sell more homes right away. The individual salespeople were able to take greater ownership of the event by setting most of the agenda themselves. They were actually the clients, and I was their personal consultant. The concept was like an athlete having a personal coach to help hone individual skills. The results in terms of increased sales were immediate and tangible. And so were the improvements in other areas of their responsibilities, such as customer management, marketing strategy, administrative responsibilities, and relationships within the company.

Soon I was working one-on-one with managers, as well, brainstorming with them as I did with salespeople, helping them provide better support systems for their salespeople. Both salespeople and sales managers liked the concept because it was positive and non-threatening. It was perceived as a true service to them as individuals. My own skills continued to improve with experience. I was able to learn skills from salespeople and managers that I could use to help others. I saw the variety of ways that challenges could be successfully handled, so I could tailor my suggestions for the different sales and management styles.

The idea continued to become more successful, so that after three years I had fulfilled my vision of doing exclusively one-on-one coaching and mentoring for companies throughout the United States. I have reached a level of personal fulfillment far beyond anything I had ever experienced in my career before, because I have been able to use my own particular creative gifts more effectively. I have the rich enjoyment of tailoring my coaching to each customer in a different way, depending upon their own individuality—their personality, strengths, and styles as well as their unique challenges.

As I said earlier, I am no more creative than average. Yet, I can say for certain that bringing my own creative force into the process of dreaming, envisioning, planning, and executing a career has brought me a sense of fulfillment greater than I ever thought possible. I love almost every day of my work, and the ability to include my own kind of creativity in my work has enriched my life tremendously. I enjoy the fulfillment from the power to create more than I ever dreamed I would, and the enjoyment of creativity has enriched many other areas of my life as well.

As we strive to develop and exercise *The Five Powers that Lead to Fulfillment,* those of us with children can also nurture these five powers in them. We will discuss this idea more with Power #5, "The Power to Influence."

We can teach our children the importance of creativity as we recognize and encourage their efforts to be creative.

They should have as many opportunities as possible to discover and exercise their individual creativity. Two of these opportunities are school work and hobbies. Certain family activities can also focus on creativity. If we neglect this responsibility, we will be depriving our children of one of the greatest joys of living.

Creativity can be taught hand-in-hand with responsibility in order to keep the creativity on a positive, productive track. At the same time, children need the freedom to let their creativity flow and develop in its own direction.

In one sense, we sometimes consider our children to be our creation. While this is certainly true in the biological sense, we must be careful not to think of our children as clones of ourselves. If we attempt to mold our children too rigidly along the paths of our own goals and ideals, we are more likely to stifle their creativity than to enhance it. The same is true with employees, students, or anyone else we are responsible for teaching. Our goal is not to shape people, but to help them shape themselves in a positive way that will lead to personal fulfillment that is uniquely their own.

SUMMARY

The power to create is the power to add something to the world that could not have existed without you. These creations are some of your greatest sources of fulfillment.

You never need to wonder if you are creative. Know that you are; everyone is. One of the keys to achieving fulfillment is appreciating who you are and what gifts you have, and one of your gifts is creativity. If you are struggling to discover where your creativity lies, a good place to begin your search is in your own past. What have you already added to the world that has brought you satisfaction?

Chapter One discussed the importance of choice in achieving fulfillment as we choose our reaction to the events in our lives. Choice is the key to all five of our powers. Just as we can control and direct our reactions to events, and the ultimate effect of those events, we can do the same with our creativity.

In this chapter, we discussed how to search for your creativity, and discussed the following avenues through which to exercise it:

♦ Thought management—creating and taking charge of your own thought process. (Remember, your thoughts are your most frequent creation.)

♦ Creating a vision for your life.

♦ Creativity in your career.

♦ Creativity in other activities.

♦ Creativity in relationships.

♦ Creativity with children (and nurturing their creativity).

One goal of this book is to explain *The Five Powers that Lead to Fulfillment*. Another is to show how these powers work together. The next chapter will show how Power #1 ("The Power to Choose Your Reaction") and Power #2 ("The Power to Create") combine to set the stage for Power #3 ("The Power to Recreate Yourself").

3

POWER

TO

RECREATE

YOURSELF

By the time Alfred was thirty-seven, he had been with his company twelve years. His skill, commitment, and integrity had built him an excellent reputation. He had also developed an outstanding background by succeeding in every major department except accounting. He had worked at least one year each in sales, marketing, design, production, and customer service. At the age of thirty-four, he had become a division manager, and for each of the next three years his division had exceeded its goal. The next step was vice president. Everyone believed he was a shoo-in, for he was popular as well as successful. He was considered a fine manager and an excellent producer. He had the personality, the credibility, and the track record needed for the job.

Alfred had paid a price for his success, but he felt the price was worth it. He consistently worked six or seven days a week and many evenings. No one in the company at any level worked more hours a year than he. His wife was understanding, but at times frustrated. She had been an excellent mother to their daughter and son, who by this time were nine and seven years old.

Brian, the vice president whose position Alfred sought, was a good friend, and had also been an outstanding mentor. He had been preparing Alfred to succeed him in order to make his own promotion to executive vice president an easier transition. However, before that time came, Brian was offered the presidency of another company and gave his thirty-day notice.

To everyone's surprise, Sam, another division manager who was considered less qualified and less respected, was offered the promotion Alfred had expected. Alfred went to the president for an explanation, but was told only that Sam was "the right man for the job." Alfred then called Brian for his perception. Brian's response was, "I have to tell you, it was a shock to me, too. I'm not exactly sure why. They just like Sam better." Alfred never learned why Sam was given the promotion instead of him.

The incident caused Alfred to reevaluate his life. He could reduce his work week by twenty hours and still equal Sam's prior performance. The easier schedule would clearly meet the company's expectations. It would be no less than the other division managers were putting in. He would never be the type of employee to "work to the rule" just because he had been passed over. He would still produce a high level of excellence in his job, but now he would seek a different balance. He cut his work week from an average of seventy-five hours a week to about fifty-five. While his efforts did not entirely meet his previous standards, he was able to adjust his own standards to be more consistent with those of the company.

With the remaining twenty hours he now had each week, he was able to spend more time with his family and friends. His wife enjoyed their more active social life, and, to his surprise, so did Alfred. He was also able to cultivate some other interests with which he had toyed briefly in his mind but never pursued, especially hiking, astronomy, and cooking. His delight in living rose to a level he had never experienced before. He had lived a productive professional life for years. But now, for the first time, he began to understand what true fulfillment was all about.

Unlike all other creatures on earth, we have the unique power to choose who we are. For some of us, it takes a while for the wonder of this concept to sink in. Every day we get to choose who we will be. And if we don't like who we are, or if who we are isn't working out for us, we get to change it. The tricky part, of course, is making sure our change is an improvement. Like the first two powers we discussed, we must begin by realizing that the ability to recreate ourselves really is a power, and that we all have it.

One of life's greatest opportunities is the ability to start over.

Starting over does not always mean changing your circumstances, at least not right away. You may need to endure your current circumstances a while longer. This kind of perseverance may prepare you to be more successful at your next level when the opportunity does arrive. But even when you are stuck in your circumstances, you are not stuck in your identity.

What is your identity? It is what makes you different from everyone else. It is your unique spirit. Your identity includes your purpose. From time to time we ask ourselves, "What is my purpose? What am I all about?" Having a purpose is critical to our fulfillment.

As with the first two powers, we are confronted again with the issue of choice. You may not always get to choose your circumstances, but you can choose your purpose. You can choose your identity.

The first two powers are the power to choose your reaction and the power to create. The principles we discussed for getting the most out of our first two powers lead directly to this third magnificent power, the power to recreate yourself. Once you realize the magnitude of your ability to choose and to create, you see how profoundly you really can choose the way you recreate yourself.

Many people never exercise this power. After all, we are given many reasons not to exercise it or even consider it. We are told that we are stuck with who we are, or with who our parents are. Some studies claim our identity is determined by our culture. Other studies say we are determined by our circumstances and our adversities. We are taught to be victims.

Recreating ourselves is not easy. There are no short cuts or magic formulas. But once we understand our power to choose and create, we realize that our power to choose who we are is already within us, waiting to be tapped. When we consider the people we know who are most fulfilled, this is one of the most important initiatives they have taken.

Every day I work with people who have recreated themselves in a significant way. This is often an important theme in the life of a salesperson. In Chapter One, I told my own story of falling into sales by accident. Selling homes caused me to recreate myself, and the same is true for many salespeople. How many people dream of being a salesperson as a child, or study for it in school? Very few.

Beginning a career in sales normally requires a change in direction from an earlier plan. Sometimes it begins with disappointment that nothing else worked out, doubt as to whether the skills and temperament for sales are there, and fear of the unknown that lies ahead. Yet, again and again, I see salespeople discover a delight with their careers and themselves that they had never known before.

For many who enter the world of sales, recreating themselves produces fear and anxiety. But at the same time, they develop the courage and perseverance to find fulfillment in all the good that comes from the new direction they have taken.

Glass-half-empty people are less likely to succeed in new home sales over the long haul. But salespeople who look for a glass half full often find one that is running over.

How do you decide who you want to be—who you *will* be? Here are some questions to get you started. As with the questions for discovering your creativity in the last chapter, these questions overlap with one another, because the subtle differences will be more important to some people than to others. The purpose of these questions is to develop an overall thought process for deciding who you choose to be.

♦ For what do you want to be known? (What do you want people to say about you after you've passed on? What do you want people to say about you today?)

♦ What is your definition of an ideal person?

♦ What would your vision for your life be if you had no restrictions? How would this vision have to change to accommodate the restrictions that exist in your life?

♦ What do you believe is your mission or purpose in life? What would have to change in order for you to fulfill that mission or purpose? Do you have the power to make those changes, either immediately or over time?

♦ Why do you think you were created?

♦ What are your most important long-term goals? What are your most important short-term goals?

We have been taught that writing down our plans and goals is an important part of getting them to the action stage. Having your goals, direction, and vision written down is a vital part of any pursuit for fulfillment. Goals need to be specific, and they need to be something that you can envision clearly. Our visions for our goals translate into plans. Each goal should be accompanied by a plan to accomplish that goal. A goal without a plan has little chance of being achieved.

Reinventing yourself does not have to be completed today. The only thing that does have to be completed today is to begin seriously thinking about it. It may not be a matter of life or death, but it is certainly a matter of life. We are talking about drawing the map that will lead you to the buried treasure of fulfillment. It is one of the most productive investments of time you can make.

People will often spend a lot of time thinking about *what* they want to be, especially in terms of a career. Unfortunately, they often spend much less time thinking about the more important issue of *who* they want to be. You will achieve fulfillment far more successfully if you can decide who you want to be before you decide what you want to be.

Once you have answered the above questions about who you want to be, the next objective is to figure out how to get there. This may first require a close look at who you are today. Following are some questions to help gain greater insight into your current identity. Once you answer these questions, you can begin to plan the journey that will take you from who you are to who you want to be. Once again, this plan should be written.

♦ What do you think of yourself today?

♦ How do you feel you are known by others today? If they were talking about you at this moment, what do you think they would be saying? How would your biographer describe you?

♦ How does your current self compare with the person you described above that you want to be?

♦ What are your most treasured values today? Is your life consistent with those values?

♦ What are your true priorities? Does your life prove that these really are your priorities?

♦ What do you stand for? Is it clear to people around you that this is what you stand for?

♦ What is the center of your world today? When the center of our world is us, fulfillment remains beyond our grasp. Self-centeredness is a miserable and unfulfilling state of mind. Misery and depression often find their way back to pride and self-centeredness. Our lives must be about something more than ourselves.

♦ Who is your master? Whom do you serve? This question is similar to, What is the center of your world? We must honestly face the fact of who or what is our master and the center of our world. Is it a mission we believe in? Is it family? Is it money or career success? Is it the success of our children in areas that are much more important to us than to them?

Money in particular can be a powerful master, as well as a destructive one. (We will discuss this more in our next chapter on the power of giving.)

At the same time, if we feel our life has no center, then we have another problem. If it has no center, then it has no shape or direction. Choosing what will be our driving force, our center, is a very important decision we must take charge of making, before the outside world makes it for us. Our lives must have a center.

♦ What (or whom) do you fear? Whatever we fear the most is often our master and the center of our world.

As we said above, comparing your answers to the second set of questions with your answers to the first set will enable you to begin to draw your map to fulfillment. As with any map, the two points with which you start are your current location and your destination. The journey, then, becomes finding the route that connects these two points. Unlike a geographical map, the beauty of your fulfillment map is that you get to create the route in your own imagination. But, as with a geographical map, the route has no value until it is written down.

In the chapter on creativity, we discussed the importance of setting aside time to think. Creating your fulfillment map is an example of an exciting way to use this time.

You may, in fact, have a number of maps. You could have one that plans the journey from what people say about you today to what you want people to say about you in the future. Another map could plot the direction from what the center of your world is today to what you want the center of your world to be. A third map could lead from a description of your current self to a description of your ideal person. The important point is to come away from this exercise with a game plan and a timetable for moving your plan from one stage to the next.

If you are discontent with who you are today, then go through this exercise to help you decide who you want to be and how to get there. This exercise will help you create your vision, and then put together your plan for pursuing that vision and bringing it to life. At the same time, it is equally important to realize and appreciate all the qualities about yourself that are already good, valuable, and fulfilling. When you recreate yourself, be sure to recreate only the parts with which you are dissatisfied, while keeping the rest intact.

Jason made good money at the law firm in which he was a partner, but he spent more than he earned. He believed an attorney of his stature deserved the good life. Whatever debts he ran up could be paid off from his future success. Sandy, his wife, worried. She was more conservative, not the fast-lane type. Neither was Jason when they first married, but success had changed him. His desire for excitement led to an affair. His behavior was increasingly hurtful to Sandy.

As he spent more and more money lavishing his new girlfriend, his debts continued to pile up and his payments fell behind. He stole from his firm in order to keep up. His first affair ended, but others took its place. Within several years, his embezzling had climbed to over two hundred thousand dollars. His work got sloppy and he began to lose clients. His stealing got sloppy, too, and his partners caught him.

Within six months, he was serving a merciful three-year sentence. During the course of the trial, his marital indiscretions also became public knowledge, and Sandy left.

Jason served his time and came out of prison to nothing. He was now forty-four; his wife was gone; he had been disbarred. His former friends no longer wanted anything to do with him. The only profession he knew was law.

He had lived in the same town of about ninety thousand people all his life. His reputation had been destroyed, but, strangely, he decided to stay there. It was a curious decision, but one he had considered carefully while he was in prison.

For his first few months behind bars, Jason was consumed with bitterness. He felt life had dealt him a raw deal. In his hour of need, his wife, his law partners, and his friends had all deserted him, even though he believed he had always been there for them. As soon as his term was up, he would find a new town with more opportunities and people he could trust.

As Jason got to know the other inmates, he found many of them had their stories, too. However, he developed a special respect for a fellow named Ron who never made any excuses. That was not the reason Jason liked Ron at first. He just felt more comfortable being around Ron. Somehow he felt uplifted by him. Ron admitted he had done wrong, yet he did not feel he was doomed forever. He knew he could start over. It would not be easy, and he could not make right the things he had done wrong. But he could move on and still lead a positive life once he got out. It even seemed as though he was already doing that. There was a peacefulness about Ron that gave Jason hope for himself.

Jason began to rethink how he would start over. First, he faced up to the realization that he had sunk to the bottom of the human barrel. He had become a rotten person, and people who depended on him had paid a price for it. They were the ones who had gotten the raw deal, not him. When he got out, he could not be the same person he had been before. He began to realize that for his life to have value, he would need to recreate himself. He would probably never reach the level of prosperity he once had, but perhaps this was a blessing. He could still be successful, although it would have to be in much different, more important ways. But how would he achieve this success? What would he be? What opportunities would be open to him? He would use the next two and a half years to begin his new direction. It seemed to be working for Ron.

Jason realized that before he could decide what he would be when he got out, he would first have to decide who he would be. Certainly not the person he was. But who? He began to ask himself the tough questions. What would people say about him if he died today? What would he want people to say about him once he had the opportunity to show people he had recreated himself? For what did he want to be known? What kind of person did he want to be? Was there anything about his former self that he wanted to preserve?

He wanted to keep his drive for success, but he wanted to redirect it in a more positive and meaningful direction. He wanted to have a purpose beyond simply himself. His whole purpose had previously been himself. Maybe that was even the root of his other troubles. Now he began to consider that if he made his purpose something bigger, he would be taken care of in the process. It would simply happen. He wouldn't have to worry about it. He could worry about more important things, things that really made a difference.

What kind of a job would he have? He realized this was probably something he could not control—at least not for a while. In the beginning, his opportunities would be limited. But perhaps that was not the most important thing. If he could recreate himself into the kind of person that matched his new ideal, the right job might not be such an issue. But what was that ideal? He began to create a vision of himself as he wanted to be.

Jason decided that he wanted to be known as a person who had done everything wrong that could possibly be done wrong, and then had been redeemed. He wanted to be a person who could provide hope to people who had lost their hope—someone who could provide inspiration in the face of adversity. That would be his mission, his purpose. Perhaps that is why he had been created in the first place—to walk the path he had walked in order to be able to provide that unique kind of hope and guidance. Maybe the best part of his life was ahead of him after all—his first real opportunity to make a difference in a significant and positive way. He could help others redeem lives that seemed doomed to destruction. And what better place to start than in a prison?

Jason moved the center of his world and decided to choose a new master. His center and his master would no longer be himself, his success, and his money. It would be something far greater.

As the rest of his first year passed, Jason focused on getting to know other inmates. He grew interested in them as individuals and in anything they were willing to share about themselves. He also became more open about himself. He talked about the mistakes he had made and how he needed to turn himself around in order to create a life worth living. He treated the other inmates with more respect. Even those he disliked, he would not criticize behind their backs. Respect is easy to reciprocate. As a result of treating those around him with respect, he received respect in return. Over the remaining two years, his attitude and demeanor seemed to catch on. Respect was something almost everyone there wanted and valued when they got it.

Gradual and subtle changes began to occur. Inmates became more willing to exchange ideas. They realized they could enrich themselves in their present environment just by being willing to share more of themselves and to encourage each other. An atmosphere of respect and encouragement started to develop, and then evolved into an atmosphere of hope.

When Jason was released, many inmates expressed their gratitude for his friendship. Several of the guards and even the warden expressed similar sentiments. He knew he would be missed. His final two years in prison had brought him more fulfillment than any time in his life up to that point. But he was ready to move on.

He had already decided that recreating himself would mean going back to his hometown, even though it would be the toughest environment he could possibly face. It would be more difficult than what he had faced in prison.

He was right. The hostility was devastating. Sandy had moved away, but his partners and most of his former friends remained. Many people showed they were still as disgusted with him as they had been when he left. They were shocked that he would ever show his face there again, let alone come back to live. The anger and outrage did not seem to have diminished at all with time.

He began going quietly to each of the people he had wronged to express his remorse and show the sincerity of his repentance. He explained that he had come back rather than run in order to take responsibility for what he had done and face the consequences of his actions head on. He asked each person to forgive him. It went pretty well with some, less well with others. The law firm had survived. His girlfriends had moved on with their lives. The only person he had truly devastated was Sandy. He got her phone number from one of her relatives in another town who was sympathetic to his sorrow. He spoke to her only once. She told him she never wanted to see or hear from him again. She refused to tell him what she was doing. She had severed all ties, kept an unlisted number, and answered no letters. He knew now that he would have to live with the sorrow and regret of that void for the rest of his life.

He lived in an apartment for several months on money from his parents. They lived far away, but they told him they still loved him and wanted to help him get back on his feet as long as he was sincere. They offered him a place to live, but understood his reasons for trying to start over again in his old town.

For four months, Jason was unable to find work of any kind. Finally a new friend named Clark decided to take a chance on him. Clark owned a hardware store and hired Jason to handle the stock and perform occasional clerk duties. Jason was industrious, and the store's business did not drop off as a result of his being there. Customers who had never known Jason before liked him. His aptitude for business and desire to succeed helped make the store more successful, so Clark continued to give him more responsibility. Within five years, Clark was able to open a second store on the other side of town. Jason became manager of the first store. He had done a good job, made a positive contribution, and was satisfied with the life he led. His deepest satisfaction came from volunteer work in a poor section of town.

When he was forty-nine, he married a childhood friend named Claire. She had also been previously married and had three grown children. They never had any more children, but Jason loved Claire dearly and faithfully. Ironically, she worked in a law office, but that was never a problem. Jason had become accepted as the person he had envisioned. He had truly recreated himself.

Redemption is a glorious triumph and a wondrously fulfilling experience. In Chapter One, we discussed comebacks. Redeeming ourselves from a devastating failure or humiliation is the most difficult form of comeback and possibly the greatest. It is perhaps the highest example of using the power to recreate ourselves.

To redeem one's self is heroic. It requires extraordinary courage, the type of courage Jason demonstrated by facing a hostile hometown instead of going somewhere else to start over. In some cases, going to a new place would have been the better decision. What made Jason's case different was that his vision for himself demanded that he start over in the same place where he had faced his downfall and humiliation. That was the best place to show the true power of redemption—the power to recreate himself, which was part of his vision.

When we hit rock bottom, enduring failure, humiliation, and condemnation, thoughts about the future can sometimes lead to profound despair. When we reach those times that we feel we have no place left to go with our lives, the ability to start over—to recreate ourselves—can be one of the most magnificent parts of the human experience. We cannot always recreate our circumstances, but we can recreate our spirit. This is what Jason did.

Self-love is an important ingredient in the formula for fulfillment. By self-love, I do not mean conceit, but an unconditional commitment to caring for, accepting, and forgiving yourself. This is the same kind of unconditional love you would feel for another person.

In the chapter on "Choosing Your Reaction," we talked about forgiveness. Redemption begins with forgiveness of ourselves. Forgiveness and redemption go hand in hand, whether we forgive ourselves or are forgiven by someone else.

Our contentment is a choice, and our happiness is our responsibility. Self-forgiveness, therefore, is often a strong act of will, not simply a response to the emotion of guilt. In self-forgiveness, we force ourselves to let go of our baggage by realizing that guilt is self-destructive. Guilt is not the same as responsibility. We forgive ourselves the same way we forgive someone else. In self-forgiveness, we realize that true repentance wipes the slate clean so that we can begin again and recreate a better self.

What about forgiveness from others? In order to move on with our lives, we must ask forgiveness, assuming it will be given if our repentance is sincere. People can relate to imperfection. What they want to see is behavior that proves the repentance and desire to improve are genuine.

Repentance holds a connotation of honor. It is the opposite of a cover-up. We all have our blunders and humiliations on which to look back. Most people like to see comebacks, just as they root for underdogs. We admire the idea of people rising from their own ashes to overcome adversity, and we admire heroes who overcome adversity with honor and courage.

Most people don't want to spend their lives being angry with you. Hopefully, they have more important issues on which to focus. However, if someone refuses to forgive you, then your self-forgiveness will have to be enough. Prove to yourself, to the offended party, and to the rest of the world that your redemption is real. The other person's failure to forgive becomes their burden to bear, not yours. We discussed this same principle in reverse in Chapter One when we talked about releasing ourselves from the offenses of others through forgiveness.

Recreating yourself requires the kind of long-term, big-picture thinking we discussed earlier. With redemption, we go back to the issue of choosing who we want to be or how we want to be known. After suffering disgrace for wrongdoing, we can become someone who used adversity for good—who came back and made a positive difference greater than our transgression.

The key to redemption is the desire to help others. People who help others are the real heroes who stand the test of time, as long as their motives do not become corrupted.

Unfortunately, when we hit hard times, we tend to look inward when we should be looking outward. It is ironic that in situations where we have the greatest need to recreate ourselves in a positive way, we instead become more focused than ever on merely looking out for ourselves. Our own well-being becomes the center of our world.

In reality, it is the opposite course of action—looking outward beyond ourselves to the bigger picture—that is the path to redemption and the key to fulfillment.

Summary

The fulfillment you achieve will result partly from your ability to be who you want to be. How you perceive yourself and whether you believe your life has value affects everything else you think, feel, and do.

Chapter Two discussed your power to create, including the creation of a vision for your life. Your greatest creation of all is yourself. You have the power to choose your own identity, what makes you different and special. You can choose your purpose in life. Just as you can create yourself, you can also recreate yourself.

In creating or recreating yourself, it is more important to decide *who* you want to be than *what* you want to be. You may not always be able to choose your career, but you can always choose your identity, your purpose, and your character. Those are the areas where true fulfillment lies.

By combining the power to choose your reaction with the power to create, you develop the power to recreate yourself. While Chapter Two explained how to create a vision for your life, the current chapter described how to recreate yourself by creating a fulfillment map. Drawing this map begins by answering the questions listed in this chapter for self-examination and then for setting a direction to your new destination.

As with any map, you are restricted by the terrain of your existing circumstances. The terrain around you may affect the details of your journey and the time it takes to reach your destination. But the quality of your journey is still your choice.

We each have a different life and a different map. Our lives, maps, experiences, and creativity are uniquely our own. It is important not to squander precious energy on jealousy over the outward appearance of someone else's life. We each travel our journey in a different way, at a different speed, across different terrain. Life is a series of adventures, each leading to the next. We need to play out our whole story in order to know where it is really leading. This takes perseverance, patience, and a basic belief that the pieces of our life's puzzle will come together over time.

Sometimes we make mistakes, and sometimes those mistakes reduce us to humiliation. The power to recreate ourselves includes the power to redeem ourselves following humiliation, disgrace, or disastrous failure. Redeeming ourselves begins by forgiving ourselves. We then choose how we will move on by using the adversity for future good, as we recreate ourselves by looking not just inward to ourselves, but outward to the world we have the opportunity to serve.

Is life fair? We don't know that yet. A golfer can hit an excellent shot that rolls into a bad lie, while his opponent may hit an inferior shot that winds up in better position. Yet the bad lie may cause the first golfer to change his swing in a way that winds up producing a better shot than the second golfer with the easier lie.

We all play it where it lies in life. A bad lie can have a good result, and a good lie can have a bad one. So which was really the good lie after all? We cannot always choose where our shots will land, but we can always choose how to play our next shot.

Life is not a walk. It is a series of jumps and stumbles. Life's rhythm is not even, nor is it predictable. It is a package deal. We do not get to pick the best from our package and the best from someone else's. The glass-half-full person sees the opportunity to recreate ourselves as one of life's greatest gifts and one of our greatest powers that lead to fulfillment.

4

POWER

TO

GIVE

One of the companies with whom I work has taught me some valuable lessons about giving. The names have been changed, but the details will be accurate.

Phil, the sales manager, carried a workload that would require two or three managers in most companies. Many managers would find neither the time nor the energy to do much giving in a situation like Phil's. Yet his top priority continued to be the well-being of his salespeople. While he could never spend as much time with them as he wanted, they always knew he was there if they needed him. He would put his other work aside and work later into the evenings or on his days off in order to give his salespeople the support they needed. Even when he was under the greatest pressure, he never lost his loving demeanor. He remained kind and gentle with his salespeople. He could still be a no-nonsense manager when he had to, but everyone knew his top priority was to do the right thing.

Randy was the company's most successful salesperson. Like Phil, Randy was tough when he needed to be, but he provided valuable support to his co-workers. He was intensely competitive, yet he also saw the bigger picture. He helped the newer salespeople even when it meant they might beat him in sales for the month.

Despite an overly competitive market that created a difficult selling environment for all the builders in the area, morale in Phil's sales department was always high. The salespeople knew they were appreciated and respected, and they gave the credit for the upbeat atmosphere to Phil and Randy. The two leaders worked together to make sure there was enough attention and support to go around, even in the face of Phil's unrealistic workload. In the giving environment Phil and Randy had created, the few mistakes that either of them made were easy for everyone else to forgive.

As significant as the high morale was the fact that sales and profits in that company were extraordinary for their marketplace. Every salesperson in the company was very successful under challenging market conditions. It was gratifying to see how a sales department that was focused on respect, support, and giving could produce profits as well as happiness.

Giving is one of the most uplifting joys you can experience. When you reflect on the excitement and satisfaction that comes from the joy of giving, it is easy to see that giving is one of the roads that lead to fulfillment. However, you must make sure you are on the right road. It is joyful giving that paves the road to fulfillment. Reluctant giving takes you in the opposite direction.

Reluctant giving would include charitable gifts you feel coerced or forced into giving. This kind of giving is frustrating and leaves you with a bad taste in your mouth about the whole idea of giving. There is no fulfillment when you give in order to relieve anxiety, pressure, or guilt, because that is not true giving. When giving is nothing more than the path of least resistance, it brings neither joy nor fulfillment. The giving that produces excitement and joy comes when you give simply because you believe in the cause and want to give. Giving from the heart leads to fulfillment.

Just as there is a difference between reluctant giving and giving from the heart, there is also a distinction between helpful giving and harmful giving. Giving money to an alcoholic to buy more liquor is quite different from paying for a treatment program for him. When giving is motivated by a desire to serve rather than to escape, and when you believe your gift will make a difference, even a small one, you realize you have value in the world. This is fulfillment.

If giving brings us joy and fulfillment, why are we so ambivalent about it? Why doesn't everyone give freely?

All five of the powers discussed in this book seem very simple, yet we struggle with conflicting feelings about each of them. We sometimes choose reactions that are harmful to us as well as to others. We deny or misuse the power to create and to recreate ourselves. The first three chapters discussed choices that involve reacting, creating, and recreating ourselves. Now let's look at the choices that involve giving.

One of the forces working against the desire to give is the desire to accumulate. For many people, financial net worth is an important part of their identity. It is a means of measuring success. Studies of net worth statistics set a standard for comparison. If people see they are above average, it gives them a feeling of excitement and confidence. If they are below average, it can cause anxiety and self-doubt. They fear that giving could push them down even further.

Net worth can be confused with value, just as gratification can be confused with fulfillment. Accumulation can certainly be very gratifying, at least for awhile. But accumulating does not bring the fulfillment that giving brings.

Revering net worth can be dangerous. At the superficial level, net worth can be perceived as a measure of success. But at a deeper level lies the haunting thought that our net worth is also the sum total of everything we could have given but chose to hoard. This is not to say that having a large net worth is wrong. It can be a very legitimate symbol of a successful career or of wise investment choices. It can support a comfortable lifestyle (at least materially) which is honestly earned and deserved. A large net worth is not a bad thing to have, but it is a sad thing to worship. The ability to accumulate may lead to material comfort, but it does not lead to fulfillment. The power to give leads to fulfillment. The power to give can be a more important measure of someone's true worth than their power to accumulate. The power to give releases your true worth for the world to appreciate.

One of the great satisfactions of giving comes from knowing that you actually have something worth giving. Ask yourself, "What do I have that is worth giving? What do I have that will improve the lives of others? What do I have that will make a difference?"

Accumulating is an investment in the material world. Giving is an investment in the spiritual world—the world in which our soul resides. Giving liberates us from the bondage of the material world. It raises us above the entire net worth hierarchy. It frees us from the bondage of greed, possessions, and selfishness in the same way that forgiveness frees us from the bondage of anger and envy.

Some people are primarily givers by nature, while others are primarily takers. Takers evaluate life situations in terms of what's in it for them. They extract what they can and move on. They are frequently manipulative in their tactics. The well-being of others becomes important only when it is convenient. If helping others will help the taker as well, then he becomes benevolent. Otherwise, there is no point.

Givers live more fulfilled lives than takers. Takers suffer an emptiness wherever they go. The life of the taker is a prison of anxiety over not having enough. The giver is released from that prison.

Some people achieve fulfillment by using the power to recreate themselves to change from takers to givers. Their purpose in life is elevated, and their lives are enriched as they enrich the lives of others.

The power to give also relates to the power to choose our reaction and the power to create. We can use the power to choose our reaction to decide whether we will be givers or takers under the pressure of adversity. We can use our power to create to choose whether our creations will be merely for ourselves or for others as well.

Giving is also part of the big-picture, long-term thinking we discussed in earlier chapters. Giving raises our lives to that higher level of living for something beyond ourselves.

Included within the power to give is the power to sacrifice.

Why do I call sacrifice a power? For the same reason I call giving a power. It is a choice you can make that will increase the value of your life.

Giving may or may not require sacrifice. When giving causes you to inconvenience or deprive yourself, then it becomes sacrificial giving. A giving spirit is necessary in order for sacrifice to produce fulfillment. A sacrifice made only after determining "what's in it for me" will not reap the same level of fulfillment as a sacrifice for the good of someone else or for a higher cause.

In a practical sense, sacrifice can also have tangible personal benefits. In my work with salespeople and managers, I try to understand what makes some more successful than others. I see one pattern repeatedly. One of the most significant factors in success (more than intelligence, talent, or even hard work and commitment) is the willingness to make sacrifices, to do things that other people are unwilling to do. I am talking not only about the extra hours it may take to do a better job, but also about doing the tasks that are unpleasant yet necessary. This includes responsibilities that are often "beneath" the employee's official job description, as well as those that offer no reward or recognition. Sometimes these tasks even benefit another employee more than the one making the sacrifice. Again, it takes long-term, big-picture, glass-half-full thinking to make these kinds of sacrifices.

One of the best new home salespeople I ever knew was committed throughout his career to the principle of sacrifice. He gave a consistently high level of professional service to his co-workers in the sales and construction departments, to his managers, and to his customers. He treated the field workers with the same respect he gave to the owners of the company. He was frequently the one to pick up the slack while others were saying, "It's not my job." Yet, he did not let co-workers or customers walk on him. When the correct answer was no, he said no. But even then, he would always give a complete and respectful explanation. When he assisted his managers or co-workers, he frequently let them take all the credit for the success.

In addition to sacrificing time and recognition to help those around him become more successful, he also sacrificed potential commissions by helping other salespeople make sales that could have been his. The fulfillment he gained from his career came more from what he gave than what he earned. And he earned a lot, for he was one of the company's top producers year after year.

This salesperson was truly a glass-half-full, big-picture thinker. He derived tremendous satisfaction from his career in addition to his success. His attitude and reputation also gained him promotions. He became a general sales manager, and later a vice president. His willingness to sacrifice gained him respect and success in management as it did in sales. The sales team he managed became the most successful team in terms of average volume per salesperson of any home builder in the their market.

The extra time he had invested in getting the job done and helping others to succeed paid off handsomely. The losses of money and recognition he incurred from his sacrifices were repaid with huge dividends.

As with other types of giving, sacrifice can produce ambivalent feelings. Doubts are raised by questions such as these: Am I being taken advantage of? Is this going to pay off? Is the sacrifice really worth it? Will I be sorry later? Will I be forced to miss an opportunity? Is it fair? Is it right?

While these types of questions may be valid, the larger point is that sacrifice is another way of giving that produces a positive impact on the world around you. Sacrifice is not just a rip-off; it is a very high calling which produces a high level of fulfillment.

Seeking fulfillment through giving can begin by asking ourselves three questions:

1. What (or how) can we give?

2. When (or where) can we give?

3. To whom (or what) can we give?

Let's take a look at question number one. Discussing how we can give will also help us discover answers to the other two questions. Here are some of the kinds of giving that can lead to fulfillment.

Money

The most familiar gift is money. Giving from your excess, as opposed to hoarding it, is a worthy calling. Sacrificial giving is a higher calling still. This kind of giving, as discussed earlier, can offer freedom from the prison of feeling that we never have enough money. Some people find that when they freely give money that could have brought greater comfort or pleasure for themselves, they discover a joy greater than any joy the money itself could have brought them. It gives their lives and labors a value beyond themselves.

In a small way, some people gain a glimpse into the joy and fulfillment of sacrificial giving when they give a pint of blood during a blood drive, when they don't even know who they are helping.

Naturally, sound judgment should enter into decisions to give sacrificially. Reckless giving is different from sacrificial giving. Giving a pint of blood on the same day you run an Olympic race would be foolish. Giving blood after the race is over is sacrificial without being foolish.

Time And Effort

Gifts of time and effort are perhaps the second most familiar form of giving. Even if the effort is one which delights you, such as volunteering to teach a weekend class on a topic you enjoy, gifts of time and effort are almost always sacrificial. After all, the same time and effort could usually have been devoted to a more selfish pursuit. Any pleasure gained from giving time and effort is richly deserved, but is merely a supplement to the more profound fulfillment which sacrificial giving produces.

TALENT AND GIFTS

In Chapter Two, we discussed the importance of understanding your own creativity. Just as important is understanding your unique talents and gifts. Talents and gifts offer another opportunity to enrich others and to achieve your own fulfillment. Everyone is gifted. People who appear to be more gifted than others have perhaps done a better job of identifying and developing their gifts and finding positive uses for them. Many people are gifted but do not nurture and maximize their gifts. This leads to a situation like the tree falling in the forest. If no one is around to hear it, does it really make a sound? If someone has a gift but does not identify it, develop it, or use it, are they really gifted?

To determine what your gifts are and how to make the best use of them, an exercise similar to the one we discussed in Chapter Two for creativity may be helpful.

◆ In what ways have you shown evidence of a talent or gift in the past?

◆ Did the use of your talents produce any benefit to others?

◆ Did the use of your talents produce fulfillment for you?

◆ What sort of activities bring you the kind of fulfillment that would make you believe you are gifted? In what ways have other people told you that you are gifted?

♦ How can you find more opportunities to use your gifts? What can you do to develop your gifts further?

LOVE

Love can be the hardest gift of all to give, or at least to give in a way that produces fulfillment. The "what's in it for me" approach to love leads to despair. Sacrificial love leads to fulfillment. Sacrificial love is unconditional love that exists for the purpose of service. This love does not have to be reciprocated in order to produce fulfillment, because it is a love devoid of selfishness.

CARING

There is a distinction between caring and love. Caring can be the most important kind of giving. Of all the things you can give, caring is needed universally. Caring encompasses many other forms of giving, including encouragement, sympathy, patience, listening, or just being there.

Knowing that someone cares can be enough to produce feelings of hope and worth that keep people going through their darkest hours of despair. Caring can dramatically change the course of another person's life. Over the course of a lifetime, a caring person can have an enormous impact and find enormous fulfillment in the process.

FRIENDSHIP

Friendship naturally overlaps with other forms of giving already discussed on this list. Yet it is still a separate item, because it requires a special kind of commitment. While love and caring certainly play a part in friendship, the commitment aspect of friendship is especially important.

COUNSEL

Giving counsel begins with caring. It is different than simply telling other people what to do or trying to control someone else's life. A counselor is not a puppeteer. Giving counsel begins with careful listening, and then asking questions that contribute to your mutual understanding of the issues. You use your experience and wisdom to help others develop their own thought process, so they can pursue a course of thought and action that will help them get where they are trying to go. Sometimes this means giving advice, and sometimes it means not giving advice. Sometimes it stops with listening and caring, and not offering guidance that is beyond your own horizon of understanding. Sometimes all the person wants is for you to listen. Your listening may help them organize their own thoughts and pursue a direction they decide upon for themselves.

Mentoring is another type of counseling. In private or professional life, mentoring is an important way to help people develop the thoughts and skills necessary to pursue their own success. In mentoring, we make a one-on-one commitment to help another person on a continuing basis. We are by his side as he perseveres. We use our experience, knowledge and friendship to guide the other person, and our caring to pick him up when he falls.

Counseling may include encouragement, admonishment, and sometimes both together. Counseling must be caring, patient, and always honest.

Honest encouragement is something most people need more than they get, in both their personal and professional lives. At the same time, false encouragement can cause harm by leading a person further down the wrong path. In any event, balancing encouragement, admonishment, and sensitivity can enable us to help others along the path to their fulfillment as we follow the path to our own.

OUR LIVES

In many respects, our lives are, of course, the greatest tangible possession we can give. It is a gift so huge that many of us cannot begin to comprehend the concept. Perhaps this is because as our society continues to advance in technology and material wealth, we have begun to lose our grasp of big-picture, long-term thinking. Our whole concept of giving has become skewed. The "what's in it for me" mentality runs headlong into the concept of giving our lives. When we give our lives, it is because we place something above ourselves. If we put nothing above ourselves, then the concept of giving our lives becomes nonsense. The belief that nothing is greater than ourselves is one of the obstacles that puts fulfillment beyond our grasp.

SUMMARY

The power to give leads us to fulfillment by raising our lives to the higher level of living for something beyond ourselves. It frees us from the bondage of the material world. Givers are happier, more fulfilled people than takers. Along with distinguishing between givers and takers, this chapter also discussed the difference between joyful giving and reluctant giving. Joyful giving is giving from the heart—the kind of giving that brings fulfillment.

Giving can be hampered by the fear that when you are giving, you are losing. But what you gain by giving is much greater than what you lose.

You gain fulfillment from knowing you have something worth giving. Giving is one of the most important ways you can have a positive impact on the world around you.

We discussed accumulation and net worth. There is certainly nothing wrong with accumulating wealth. It simply has no positive impact on the world, and therefore does not produce the same kind of fulfillment that giving does.

Joyful givers enjoy an abundance mentality. They believe that whatever it is they are giving, there is enough to share, with blessings to both the giver and the receiver. Takers, as well as reluctant givers, suffer the burden of a scarcity mentality.

Once again we are talking about the role of choices in the powers that lead to fulfillment. Giving is a choice. We choose to give or to take. We choose between an abundance mentality and a scarcity mentality. The choice of a life driven by fear of loss over a life filled with the joy of giving is a choice to live a life of thirst when the well of fulfillment is right in front of us.

Within the power to give, sacrifice produces a special level of fulfillment. The willingness to sacrifice is also one of the most important ingredients in the recipe for a lifetime of long-term success. In my work with salespeople and managers, I have been impressed by how often a pattern of sacrifice has been connected to a pattern of success. I have also been inspired by the fact that salespeople who are givers tend to be more successful and fulfilled over the long term than salespeople who are takers.

This chapter provided an overview of a variety of different kinds of giving that produce fulfillment:

♦ Money

♦ Time and Effort

♦ Talents and Gifts

♦ Love, Caring, and Friendship

♦ Counsel

♦ Our Lives

Joyful giving (giving from the heart) is energizing. A giving spirit produces an inner peace. People who are takers by nature often assume that giving makes them vulnerable and diminishes their resources. In fact, the opposite is true. Giving produces a different kind of strength and confidence that takers will never enjoy. It is called fulfillment.

Does giving make us poorer? Certainly not in spirit. But even in net worth, the loss is not what we think. What difference does it really make where we rank on the percentile scale of net worth? How much is enough?

Our ultimate net worth will be measured, by others and inevitably by ourselves at the deeper fulfillment level, by how much we give rather than how much we take. Understanding this truth makes giving one of our powers that lead to fulfillment.

The power to give comes together with the first three powers (choosing how things affect us, creating, and recreating ourselves) to pave the way for Power #5, "The Power to Influence."

5

POWER

TO

INFLUENCE

The story of Joseph in the Old Testament provides remarkable insights into the meaning of influence—what it is, how it is gained, and how it should be used. Joseph's story illustrates how one person used his own five powers to achieve a high level of fulfillment and an important place in history.

Joseph suffered extraordinary adversity again and again—enough to destroy the will, hope, and faith of many of us. Yet his response to adversity (Power #1) paved the road to his ultimate success and fulfillment.

His most difficult trials began when he was seventeen. His brothers hated him so much they wanted him out of their lives. Not only did they dislike Joseph, their animosity was compounded by the fact that he was their father's favorite son. At first they planned to kill him, but then decided to sell him to merchants who would in turn sell him as a slave in Egypt. The Egyptian who bought Joseph was Potiphar, a captain of Pharaoh's guard.

God was the central focus of Joseph's life. His profound belief that God's plan was ultimately good shaped his thoughts, feelings, and direction. His father was Jacob, his grandfather was Isaac, and his great-grandfather was Abraham, the father of the nation of Israel. Joseph's faith enabled him to see his adversity in the context of God's love and protection. Joseph was a long-term, big-picture thinker. He had a glass-half-full mentality.

Using the power to choose his reaction, Joseph accepted his adversity as an opportunity—not one he wanted, but one he could use. Joseph chose to believe that if his God allowed the adversity, then it must have value, even if he could not yet understand it. While Joseph was clearly the victim of a terrible injustice, he assumed the injustice would turn out to be a springboard instead of an anchor.

Using the power to recreate himself, he decided that if he were destined to be a slave, he would be the best slave he could be.

As a teenager, Joseph had displayed a gift of prophecy, which further infuriated his brothers. While it may have appeared that this gift would be the primary source of his creativity, in slavery he sought out other creative outlets. He found he was creative as an administrator.

He devised organizational systems so effectively that Potiphar promoted him to the position of manager over all his personal affairs and his other employees. As Joseph's management career prospered, so did Potiphar. Joseph showed he was a good manager, and a good person.

His power to give came into play. He did not have material possessions to give, nor did Potiphar need them. What Joseph gave to Potiphar was his best effort and talent, and he gave it with a true servant's heart. Potiphar entrusted Joseph with greater responsibilities. He also grew fond of him personally.

Unfortunately, Potiphar's wife also grew fond of Joseph. She tried repeatedly to seduce him, but he would not give in. Angry over Joseph's rejection, she convinced her husband that Joseph had tried to seduce her.

Potiphar not only fired Joseph from his position as manager, but also had him thrown into prison. Even after all the good he had accomplished as Potiphar's chief steward, Joseph again became the victim of cruel injustice.

Once more he had to start over. Each time he was forced to begin again, it seemed to be from a lower position than where he had started the previous time.

I cannot imagine the sense of futility and frustration Joseph must have felt. Not only must his faith have been stretched to the limit, but so must his sanity. Yet, his attitude did not seem to waver. He maintained his belief that the plan God had created for him was the plan that was truly best for him.

As he had done with Potiphar, Joseph gained the trust and respect of the prison keeper. Eventually, the prison keeper turned over to Joseph the responsibility for the other prisoners and for the day-to-day operations of the prison. Yet, Joseph was still a prisoner himself.

While in prison, he was joined by Pharaoh's chief butler and chief baker, who had both fallen out of favor with the king. One night they each had dreams that troubled them. After years as a slave and a prisoner, Joseph was finally given the opportunity to use his gift of prophecy again. He told the butler his dream meant that in three days he would be released from prison and restored to his previous position. He told the baker he would also be released, but he would then be hanged.

Joseph interpreted both dreams correctly. Now that the chief butler was back in Pharaoh's employment, perhaps Joseph could hope for a better future. All the butler had to do was tell the story of Joseph's prophecy to Pharaoh, and it would mean good news for Joseph. But the butler did not mention the incident, so Joseph stayed in prison.

By this time, Joseph was twenty-eight years old. For eleven years he had been unfairly victimized. If we call his circumstances luck, he had a miserable run of it for a long time. Through all this time, he chose his reactions (Power

#1) believing that each of his setbacks were part of God's long-range plan for him. He employed his creative skills (Power #2) as each situation required. He recreated himself (Power #3) in the way that would maximize the opportunity that lay within each challenge he faced. And he continued to maintain the spirit of a giver (Power #4), not a taker.

After he lost his credibility with his brothers, he regained it with Potiphar. After he lost it with Potiphar, he regained it with the chief of the prison. He faithfully maximized the opportunity of each day without getting caught in the trap of making himself the center of his world. Because he was never the center of his world, his adversities never produced self-pity. He was able to keep moving forward toward fulfillment, no matter what his circumstances were. He continued to look beyond himself, first to the God who was the center of his world, and then to whomever he could serve on any given day.

Two years later, at the age of thirty, and after thirteen years as a slave and a prisoner, Joseph's greatest opportunity finally came. Pharaoh had two dreams that distressed him deeply. He sent out word that he wanted someone who could interpret them. Many who claimed that ability responded, but no one could make any sense out of the dreams. Finally, the chief butler came forward with the story of his experience with Joseph in prison. Pharaoh called Joseph out of prison, and Joseph was able to interpret Pharaoh's dreams. He told Pharaoh the two dreams went together and were a gift from God predicting the next fourteen years in the history of Egypt. For the first seven years, Egypt would prosper. But the following seven years would produce a terrible famine that would threaten the entire country.

Joseph drew upon his power to create. He composed a plan to manage all resources accumulated in the prosperous seven years in order to provide for the lean seven. Pharaoh was so impressed by Joseph's insight and his plan that he released Joseph from prison and made him second in command over all of Egypt.

Each setback in Joseph's life had paved the way for the next success. Although he did not understand the reasons for his trials, each injustice moved him closer to his ultimate victory. Through continuous use of the first four powers that lead to fulfillment, he developed Power #5, the power to influence. Even when a setback caused his influence to decline in one place, he used his powers to increase it somewhere else.

Throughout his adversities, as well as his successes, he never put himself at the center of his universe. For this reason, he never lost his big-picture perspective or his glass-half-full mentality. He continued to view his challenges as springboards. He continued to create, to recreate himself, and to give. He always looked beyond himself. In this way, he continued to build influence, and he continued to achieve fulfillment.

His primary focus remained on the God he knew would love, guide, and protect him. His secondary focus was then placed on whomever God had assigned him to serve. Joseph's life was never about himself, but always something greater. Once people recognized this about him, they allowed him to have influence.

Influence is much more important than authority. In the end, Joseph had plenty of both. But his influence was always a greater power than his authority. Influence produces positive change more effectively than authority, because it has more credibility. While authority is accepted by others out of fear of the consequences, influence is accepted voluntarily. It therefore has deeper significance. Authority does not lead to fulfillment, but influence does.

We can gain tremendous wisdom from the experiences and attitudes that carried Joseph to a position of influence. His sphere of influence during his own time and throughout history has been enormous. The circumstances through which he gained his influence are even more remarkable. What are some of the lessons that are part of Joseph's extraordinary legacy?

We see once again that with a big-picture, long-term, glass-half-full mentality, we can develop the patience which allows us to understand that adversity can be the seed of victory.

In Chapter Three, you read that life is not always the steady walk we think it is supposed to be. The walk of life is more often a series of jumps, stumbles, standstills, and reversals. Our journey often does not progress in the direction nor at the speed we think it should. And yet as with Joseph, it is still possible for everything to come together and produce fulfillment.

What does it all mean?

It means that in order to keep our life moving forward (even when it appears to be moving backward), we must use our five powers for the opportunities we have today, rather than letting our powers languish in the hope that tomorrow's opportunity will be better.

From Joseph we learn that starting over is difficult, but it often raises the ultimate ceiling of our potential and our fulfillment. We learn that our lives must be focused on something higher, grander, and more important than ourselves. We find hope in this approach.

What does Joseph teach us about developing our fifth power? What is the source of true influence? How do we achieve the kind of influence that leads to fulfillment, and then how do we make the best use of that influence?

First, we see in Joseph's life how his commitment to the first four powers paved the way for him to develop the power to influence by maximizing each of his opportunities along the way.

Secondly, Joseph achieved influence throughout his life by having the heart of a servant, even when he was a master.

A servant's heart is one of the keys to achieving influence. It is also an important principle in the use of influence—that is, the kind of influence that leads to fulfillment. Misuse of influence can lead to destruction. Appropriate use of it can lead to fulfillment.

Influence is not bending other people to your will. It is helping others to maximize their own personal potential. This is how Joseph gained influence, first with Potiphar, then with the jailkeeper, then with Pharaoh, and finally by executing his plan that saved all of Egypt.

Influence is about giving, not taking. It is knowing that someone or something is better because of you. Givers usually gain true influence more easily than takers. This is an important principle in most forms of leadership. For example, managers in business who are givers have more respect, loyalty, and influence than those who are takers. It is important to distinguish between raw authority, which can extract behaviors of obedience, and true influence, which affects people on a deeper level and produces more meaningful long-term results.

In the last chapter, we discussed a variety of ways we can give. Giving can affect the kind of influence we develop, in good ways and bad. For instance, while the misuse of money, such as bribery or creating indebtedness for purposes of future control, can create negative influence, proper giving of money can produce positive influence. The first kind of influence leads to bitterness, while the second leads to fulfillment. Either way, the nature of the giving determines the nature of the influence.

Influence is also gained through the giving of time, effort, talents, love, caring, friendship, counsel, mentoring, and forgiveness.

Forgiveness was another important element in Joseph's ultimate influence over his family. As we discussed earlier, his problems began with his brothers' jealousy of him. Thirteen years later, he had legal power over them, with the authority to treat them as he pleased. Revenge would certainly have been within his rights. However, his ultimate influence within his family came from the fact that when he had the opportunity to avenge their injustice, he forgave his brothers instead. His big-picture thinking enabled him to say to his brothers, "Do not be distressed and do not be angry with yourselves for selling me here, because it was to save lives that God sent me ahead of you" (Gen. 45:5). These are the words of a person whose choices to use his five powers had brought him inner peace and fulfillment in spite of all the adversity he had survived.

My work with managers and salespeople who have gained a position of influence with their peers has taught me that the best leaders gain respect by giving respect. This does not mean good leaders contrive opportunities to give false respect when it is not earned. Good leaders look for genuine reasons and opportunities to convey respect. The respect that leaders convey must be supported by honesty and dignity—attributes critical for developing positive influence. Respect given in this way is easily reciprocated. If you want people to feel good about you, be the one who makes them feel good about themselves.

Good managers ask the question, "What can I do to make my employees better off? What can I do to enrich the lives and careers of people around me?" Enrichment, like respect, is easily reciprocated. When you show respect to those around you, you are more likely to get respect in return. When you enrich those around you, you feel more enriched by them. If you want to influence people, do something that improves or enriches their lives, not something that reduces or threatens its quality.

Influence comes from acts of kindness. We achieve influence by providing support rather than by undermining. Of course, managers must sometimes criticize or discipline people who work for them. Sometimes they must even terminate their employment if the cause is just and the action necessary. This is where the responsibility and credibility aspects of influence play a part. While managers may lose influence with a person they terminate, they gain influence in a larger sense by protecting the dignity of their other employees who have earned it. The manager is providing support and respect to those who deserve it by administering consequences to those who do not.

The most successful leaders and managers are those whose followers can say, "I'm better off because of him (or her)."

The leaders with whom I have worked that have the most influence over the long term possess the following characteristics:

AN ATTITUDE OF SELF-SACRIFICE

The leader's strength is combined with a servant's heart. The strength is seen in a willingness to persevere in the face of adversity when a principle, standard, or goal is worth defending. The servant's heart is shown in his or her willingness to be a support system as well as a boss.

A Willingness To Take Responsibility

Leaders gain credibility and respect when they are fair with themselves as well as others. This fairness includes accepting responsibility whenever it is necessary, in defeat as well as victory. It also includes holding other people responsible when appropriate. It means holding one's self as well as others accountable for mistakes, but also giving credit to those who have earned it. A good leader helps others achieve satisfaction through their accomplishments. Part of leadership is helping others achieve fulfillment. A leader's credibility can plummet if he or she takes credit for the accomplishments of someone else. Even when you have earned the credit, let others be the ones to give it to you. They will do so more eagerly if they respect your humility.

Commitment

Effective leadership requires sincere, long-term commitment. With all the ups and downs that accompany leadership, maintaining a high level of commitment can sometimes be very difficult. The best leaders remain committed to their objectives and to their people. They remain committed to the success of others. This commitment is reciprocated in the form of loyalty.

The commitment of leadership is to objectives, people, and excellence. A leader's credibility comes partly from being known as someone who pursues excellence for its own sake, and who is unwilling to compromise this commitment in the face of adversity, pressure, or politics.

Consistent Behavior

Followers need consistency from their leaders. A leader can be consistent and still be spontaneous. Consistency and spontaneity can complement each other. Consistency simply means a leader must not be erratic. The guiding principles for one day should be the same as those for the next. Followers must know where leaders stand. There is security in consistency. Consistent decisions and behavior by a leader give followers a greater sense of purpose in their own missions.

Qualities of influential leaders include characteristics we discussed previously: long-term, big-picture, glass-half-full thinking; showing respect to others; seeing beyond one's self; a calm and confident demeanor (the projection of an inner peace on the part of the leader that creates an environment of hope and security); and an environment that nurtures the goal of individual fulfillment for everyone.

Leadership is one avenue of influence. It can take a variety of forms. We often think of leadership in a military, political, or corporate sense. Teachers and ministers also fulfill a leadership role. But perhaps the most important leader of all is the parent.

One of the ways parents can provide leadership to children is to help them understand how to achieve fulfillment in life. Children can begin at an early age to appreciate the importance of making the right choices in handling the good and bad events in their lives, and the kinds of consequences these choices can have. They can learn how to explore and develop their own unique creativity. As they grow, they can learn how to adapt and recreate themselves to make the most of their changing lives. They can begin to understand the importance of giving, as well as the fulfillment that comes from a giving spirit. They can even begin to learn some of the ways they can influence others and use this influence for good. And they can be taught how to respond to influences around them. This last thought takes us full circle back to Power #1, which includes the power to make their own choices as to how they will allow themselves to be influenced. While developing the five powers is a lifelong growth process, parents can start their children on the road to fulfillment at a young age.

Leadership is not the only way to exercise the power to influence. Influence can occur in ways that are more modest, but no less important. We can influence quietly, without public glory or fanfare, one person at a time. We must not confuse publicity with influence. Influence is about making a positive difference, not about attracting attention. We do not have to be famous to be great.

It is true that actions which bring publicity may also bring influence, but this is not the same as seeking influence through publicity. Joseph achieved widespread influence and became a very high-profile celebrity. Ultimately, his influence grew into authority, which in turn further increased his influence. Yet, his influence grew first in low profile ways. It was through influence that he gained his power, wealth, and prestige—not the other way around.

Joseph achieved his success by first achieving influence. He achieved influence by having a positive impact on people around him, by simply helping people. His help took a variety of forms, from managing affairs to assuming responsibilities to interpreting dreams, whatever service he could provide for the situation at hand. His great glory came ultimately from humble acts in humbling circumstances.

So many leaders fall from grace because their desire for fame, wealth, and power perverts their desire for influence. Influence motivated by greed can sustain itself for a while, but ultimately it self-destructs. It is the motivation behind influence that determines whether the influence will last. A sincere commitment to positive influence enables the influence to survive. Influence for the sake of further personal gain will eventually deteriorate, and take fulfillment with it. History is full of people who achieved temporary influence through self-seeking means, from political leaders like Hitler to religious leaders such as Jim Jones. These kinds of leaders do have true influence for a while. But the way they pursue their influence and the kind of influence they pursue ultimately leads to destruction, not fulfillment. On a smaller scale, one-on-one influence that exists to manipulate others rather than to enrich them will also end in futility and despair.

To be sure, not all influence is good influence. As I said earlier, what we are exploring in this chapter is the kind of influence that leads to fulfillment, not the kind that leads to empty misery.

Just as influence does not have to be high profile, it also does not need to be a numbers game. We do not need to keep score of how many people we influence. Influence is about quality, not quantity. Some of the most valuable kinds of influence are those achieved on a one-on-one basis (such as mentoring) or in small groups.

Why is influence so important? How does influence lead to fulfillment? The answer to both questions is the same. Influence is what allows you to make a positive impact on the world around you, whether it is for one person or for millions. It is hard to imagine a higher calling or a greater source of fulfillment than that. In some ways, the power to influence is the culmination of the other four powers. Like the power to give, the power to influence proves that you have a worth beyond yourself. It means other people care what you think, what you do, and what you stand for. They care who you are.

Who makes up your potential spheres of influence? What kind of influence can you have within each sphere?

Family

For many people, the family is their most important sphere of influence. Failing to develop and correctly use the power to influence within that sphere can produce severe consequences.

Two important elements in developing influence within the family sphere are *communication* and *example*. These two elements work together. To neglect either will cause your level of positive influence to decline.

The most obvious route of influence within a family is the influence of parents over children. However, the family environment also needs positive influence from children to parents, between spouses, and between children. Teaching the principles of the five powers within the family will help develop the kind of positive environment in which every member of the family can pursue their own fulfillment as well as contribute to the fulfillment of other family members. Listening, helping, giving, advising, and providing support to family are all necessary in order for this sphere of influence to blossom.

These principles for gaining and using influence within the family sphere also apply to all of your other spheres of influence.

Friends

To develop influence within a friendship sphere means to provide an enriching influence, not a depleting one. Unfortunately, friendships are sometimes rooted in common grievances or misplaced sympathies. In these types of situations, especially where the theme of the friendship is commiseration rather than enrichment, friends can bring out the worst in each other instead of the best. Having positive influence with a friend requires the same kind of commitment as with a family member. It means being a springboard for that friend, not an anchor. It means combining kindness with honesty, a combination that can sometimes be difficult.

Influence is not the same as friendship. Rather than attempting to define friendship, my goal here is merely to view friendship as a sphere of influence.

Co-Workers

In a corporate environment or in any situation with a formal authority structure, we do not need authority to have influence. As we discussed earlier, authority and influence are entirely different concepts—so different that in some situations your influence can actually increase as your authority decreases.

Suppose you are a high-level manager who is demoted during a corporate takeover or restructure. While your official authority may have decreased, your actual influence can increase as you use your lower position to get closer to your co-workers. You can use the expertise you developed at the higher level to help your co-workers achieve greater success in their own positions. Your desire to make a positive difference in the lives of others causes them to allow you a role of true influence in their lives, and within the organization as a whole. Although your official leadership role has been diminished, your real position of leadership through influence has increased. You are the one to whom employees will come for advice and direction rather than the new boss. You are the one who will really make a difference, and who will achieve true fulfillment from the corporate environment.

Situations like this provide an opportunity to use all five of your powers that lead to fulfillment. You can begin by choosing the most productive reaction to the demotion—using the demotion for the good of yourself and others (even perhaps those responsible for your demotion). Next, you can use your new position to create ideas for helping yourself, others, and the company as a whole. Third, you can continue to recreate yourself within the context of your new role in order to be successful and find fulfillment in that role. Fourth, you can use your new role as a opportunity for giving. The result is a springboard for increasing your influence. This is one more example of long-term, big-picture, glass-half-full thinking. Fulfillment can be gained from any circumstances, no matter how adversarial, if you stay focused on the five powers.

VOLUNTEER GROUPS

Volunteer situations can be environments in which your influence may grow quickly. A willingness to serve, especially to do things others are unwilling to do, can create feelings of respect (as well as a sense of relief) among fellow volunteers. People in volunteer positions are often more willing to be led than they would be in professional organizations or even in families. People who take responsibility in volunteer situations can more quickly increase their level of influence. Again we see the principle of sacrifice having a payoff for the giver as well as the receiver.

AUTHORITY POSITIONS

We have already explored principles for building influence in leadership roles. These roles can be organizational, political, or religious. If leadership is a part of your own personal sphere of influence, then all the principles we discussed earlier for organizational influence, as well as those for family influence, would also apply to using your leadership authority. Even in positions of authority, selflessness is the key—and selfishness is the obstacle—to gaining influence and fulfillment.

Achieving the kind of influence that leads to fulfillment includes asking ourselves questions similar to those we have discussed earlier:

♦ What do I have to offer?

♦ What are my gifts?

♦ What is my experience?

♦ What is my expertise?

♦ How have I achieved success?

♦ How can I help others to achieve success?

♦ How do I want to be remembered?

In the big scheme of things, money, power, and titles are nothing. It is the quality of our lives (our relationships, behavior, work, accomplishments, and contributions) that determines the true value and fulfillment of our lives.

Summary

The Merriam-Webster Dictionary defines influence as "the act or power of producing an effect without apparent force or direct authority." As with the other four powers discussed in this book, the power to influence can produce fulfillment or despair, depending upon how it is used or misused. Each chapter has explored how one of the five powers can be used in ways that produce fulfillment. The kind of influence that leads to fulfillment is the kind that grows out of respect and produces lasting positive effects. It does not mean bending other people to your will, but helping them to maximize their own potential. This kind of influence begins with a servant's heart. It is about giving, not taking. Givers usually have more influence than takers. Like the power to give, the power to influence proves you have a worth beyond yourself.

Like the other four powers, the power to influence requires choices. It includes the kind of glass-half-full, long-term, big-picture thinking we have studied throughout this book.

The story of Joseph illustrates the splendor of this power. It also shows how the power to influence works together with the other four powers.

This chapter looked at the role of influence in successful leadership. Since true influence grows out of respect, we see that many successful leaders gain respect by giving respect, often through acts of kindness. We discussed other characteristics of leaders who maintain a high level of influence:

♦ An attitude of self-sacrifice

♦ Willingness to take responsibility

♦ Commitment

♦ Consistency

As with the other powers, the power to influence involves seeing beyond one's self. In leadership, it includes helping others to achieve their own fulfillment.

Leadership is only one of many spheres of influence. Other spheres include family, friends, co-workers, and volunteer groups. Our lives are filled with opportunities to exercise the power to influence and to gain fulfillment from this wonderful power.

In the end, the fulfillment we gain from each of our five powers depends not on our circumstances, our luck, or even our opportunities, but on the choices we make in determining how to use the powers to maximize the opportunities we are given. Making these choices takes honesty, courage, patience, and perseverance.

One of the greatest choices we have in life is the choice of when we will be satisfied. How much is enough? The truth is that "enough" is not a quantity at all. It is a state of mind called contentment. Contentment is a choice.

We see people who find contentment with themselves and their circumstances (and fulfillment in their lives) even in the midst of tremendous adversity. At the same time, we see other people suffering despair in the midst of prosperity and apparent good fortune. The difference between these people's level of fulfillment lies not in luck or circumstances, but in the choices they made regarding the use of their five powers. It is how we choose our reactions to the events in our lives, what we create, how we recreate ourselves to improve and enrich our lives, what we give, and the positive influence we have on the world around us that determines the fulfillment we gain through the course of our lives. One of the best pieces of advice I have ever heard was two short sentences: "Enjoy what you have. Do what you can."

Every life follows a unique path, and we must allow ourselves to be enriched by the path we follow. This book has explored ways to use the five powers we all possess in order to reach that level of contentment where we can say, "My life has been worthwhile. I'm pleased with it. It has brought fulfillment."